1996

Responses to 101 Questions on Business Ethics

George Devine

PAULIST PRESS
New York/Mahwah, N.J.

Cover designs for this series are
by James Brisson Design & Production, Williamsville, Vermont

Library of Congress Cataloging-in-Publication Data

Devine, George, 1941-
    Responses to 101 questions on business ethics / George Devine.
        p.   cm.
    Includes bibliographical references.
    ISBN 0-8091-3647-3 (alk. paper)
    1. Business ethics—Examinations, questions, etc. I. Title.
HF5387.D396 1966   96-1619
174'.4'076—dc20   CIP

Published by Paulist Press
997 Macarthur Boulevard
Mahwah, NJ 07430

Printed and bound in the
United States of America

CONTENTS

PART VII: Global Responsibility and Business Ethics

ACKNOWLEDGEMENTS

The author is grateful for the help afforded him in this process by Revs. Kevin Lynch and Richard Sparks, C.S.P., of Paulist Press, as well as the critical and constructive reaction of his students and colleagues—too numerous to name—at the University of San Francisco, in addition to the assistance of Suzanne LeGaye and Beth DeMesa in USF's McLaren School of Business with the preparation of the manuscript. Ultimately, crucial support came from the author's wife Joanne, son George and daughter Annemarie.

*This work is dedicated to those
special priests who have been,
at important times,
my link to the church:*

*Bernard F. Brennan, Jr. and
Thomas J. Burns,
of the Archdiocese of San Francisco*

INTRODUCTION

This volume hopes to be in good company with others in the "Responses to 101 Questions" series from Paulist Press.

The basic premise here is that pedagogy is moving away from a teacher-centered syllabus and toward a student-centered agenda in more and more areas of human knowledge. Notwithstanding the fact that the professor must "cover" certain bodies of data in order to properly expose some topics—the periodic table of the elements in chemistry, for instance—the fact remains that educators often make a mistake by presuming that students want to know the same things that their teachers have mastered, or that these pieces of information, often learned in a nineteenth-century academic model, will be of abiding value and utility in the third millennium.

Those who take chalk in hand these days are faced with interesting choices, even dilemmas. On the one hand, we feel charged with the responsibility to convey to our students those things (facts, theories, approaches, methods) which we have learned to be important. The longer we teach, the more we feel able to appreciate the value of things taught us in our own earlier years, for which we may have had insufficient regard at the time. Yet, we feel empathy for the young man or woman who wonders "What good is this going to do me in the real world?"

With that tension in mind, we do well to emulate the question-and-answer style which was utilized in various ways by such legendary teachers as Socrates, Thomas Aquinas and Jesus himself. This is done in an attempt to combine student inquiry with professorial responsibility to "tie it all together," all the while admitting that what is offered for many a question is not really a final answer, but the best response that can be developed at the time.

The questions and responses which follow are meant to reflect, with reasonable fidelity, the discussions held by the author with students in classes at the University of San Francisco, in his capacity as a faculty member in both the McLaren School of Business and the Department of Theology and Religious Studies in the College of Arts and Sciences, between 1989 and 1995. Some questions were submitted in writing, and some occurred in oral classroom discussion; still others arose from student reaction to preliminary drafts of this work. The sequence here is meant to preserve both the logical progression of topics and the element of spontaneity, which leads to a logic of its own.

Hopefully, we will achieve a meeting ground between the theoretical and the practical, where we will see room for some consideration of morals, ethics and law, although not always working together in the same sort of constellation in every situation. In some instances we will see a moral or ethical vision translated into law in the proper sense, in other cases we will not, and in still others we will be dealing with ethical considerations whose dimensions are not necessarily "moral" in the strict sense, although decisions of moral consequence may well be taken. That is in keeping with my point of view and experience, which I believe have merit, for this kind of study. Specifically, I am working in the context of both a philosophical and theological background and an awareness of the practicalities of modern business, embracing the operative words "business" and "ethics" that we are concerned with here.

On the one hand, I have for over thirty years been a professional student and teacher of theology, especially in the Judaeo-Christian tradition, and particularly in the atmosphere of Catholic institutions of higher learning in the United States (San Francisco, Marquette in Milwaukee, Seton Hall in New Jersey, Fordham, Manhattan and St. John's in New York) during the latter half of the twentieth century. This has surely shaped my point of view on the meaning of life and the moral norms for human behavior, based on the explicit and implicit teachings of Jesus in the New Testament, the prior foundation of the Jewish tradition in the Old Testament, and the subsequent teachings of authoritative Christian tradition. More specifically, I am a lifelong lay member of the Roman Catholic Church, which means that the tradition

I will be most influenced by will be that expressed by the popes and councils of that church. Yet my perspective is ecumenical (from the Greek *oikomene,* meaning pertaining or belonging to the whole church). This means that visions articulated by those in other parts of the Christian family (e.g., the World Council of Churches or individual religious leaders) will be important. Moreover, as a Catholic who follows the teachings of Vatican Council II (1962–1965), I value the insights of non-Christian religions, and consider myself—like many of my students and colleagues—in no small way influenced by some teachings of historic religious teachers like Confucius (*Kung-fu-tzu* or "Kung the teacher") and the Buddha ("the enlightened one" or Siddhartha Gautama).

On the other hand, I have for two decades been an active member of the business community, operating my own small family business in the stimulating atmosphere of San Francisco and engaging in regular dialogue and interaction with others in the business community. Moreover, I have been professionally involved in business education, teaching in that field as well as in theology and religious studies at a Catholic university, subsequent to having instructed for over a decade in a leading private proprietary vocational school of business in California. And I have served on two committees relative to professional ethics and business education for the state of California. This means I feel a need to spell out the practical or "nuts and bolts" application of moral principles in a way that the general terms of the bible and other religious literature are not meant to do.

My primary focus will be on the practical ethics employed by members of the business community regardless of the religious or other personal moral values held or not held by any of them. However, I don't believe this can be done in a vacuum. As I suggested before, there are some professors of ethics, and specifically business ethics, who believe they are engaging in a science of decision-making, employing a series of charts or diagrams about how choices are made. In some ways, that way of looking at things is similar to the college courses in logic or critical thinking many of us have come to know. This approach is not without value, and is often popular in the corporate culture for its emphasis on participatory process—increasingly important in the sort of diverse society we now have, with great emphasis on the dignity of the individual person. Yet we need to look inside ourselves and the others around us for values that are important to everyone in the making and implementing of decisions having ethical import.

It will be noticed at once that there are further nuances to be explored, more insights to be developed, and new questions to be answered, beyond those committed to print here. That is only natural, since human knowledge in general expands by the moment, but also because the complexities and applications of economics and ethical studies can be expected to become more complex with almost every ripple in the world's markets. What can be attempted here, then, is a redaction of the state of the questions—and the best answers that can be developed for them by the present author—at a critical point in time, upon completion of the twentieth century. And it is at times like this that I keep in mind the maxim communicated me some years ago as a participant in the Bay Area Writing Project at the University of California, Berkeley: "No piece of writing is ever finished, only abandoned!"

It will perhaps be helpful to note that the questions and responses divide as follows:

The Nature and Scope of Business Ethics

The Import and Impact of Business Ethics Today

Ethics Within Professions—A New Consciousness

Ethics in the Marketplace—Buying and Selling; Fraud and Insider Trading

Ethics in the Workplace—Obligations for Employers and Employees

Stockholders and Stakeholders—Ethical Obligations Between Companies and Communities

Global Responsibility and Business Ethics

Looking Forward: The Hint of a Conclusion

Part I

THE NATURE AND SCOPE OF
BUSINESS ETHICS

THE 101 QUESTIONS AND RESPONSES

Q. 1. Isn't "business ethics" a contradiction in terms?

This is a frequently asked question, typically the first to arise in any discussion of this kind. It doesn't have to be a contradiction in terms or an oxymoron. However, for many years people in "business" have had the reputation of needing to be ruthless in order to succeed. We've all heard remarks and jokes that perpetuate such stereotypes and caricatures, to the effect that there is no such thing as an honest person in business. And, frankly, such comments would never be made unless there were at least some truth behind them on many occasions. This sort of thing was addressed at a business oriented club I belong to, the Commonwealth Club of California, amid the scandalous atmosphere of American business in the late 1980s:

> We have all been embarrassed by recent events which make the *Wall Street Journal* read more like the *Police Gazette* with articles on bribery, bid rigging, kickbacks, and even CPAs selling their opinions. A real ethical disaster has occurred and has lowered the public's already unacceptable opinion of business behavior.

> ...This is a real tragedy, not just for those directly affected, but also for the overwhelming majority of fine, trustworthy, and honorable executives...dependent on public confidence and trust ("Ethics in Business," *The Commonwealth*, LXXXI, No. 37:398, September 14, 1987).

The speaker was J. Michael Cook, chairman and chief executive officer of Deloitte Haskins & Sells, and chairman of the board, American Institute of Public Accountants. Many, I fear, would not only agree with Mr. Cook's remarks, but perhaps even suggest that he understated the case!

We all know examples of people in business who have done things we consider dishonest, repugnant and socially irresponsible, all for the sake of personal monetary or material gain—and, in many cases, gotten away with it so far as the law is concerned. In fact, so many have done things like this that people who wish to be honest in the business world are often demoralized, and tempted to believe that they, too, must be sneaky, deceitful or dishonest in order to pay their expenses and make a decent profit. Some fine people even leave the world of business altogether and find other ways to earn a living, typically in "service professions." When they do this, they usually become employees of other people who have to make the decisions and value judgments. Those who make this kind of transition frequently say they want to avoid the trials and conflicts of business and the ethical dilemmas that often arise. It has come to the point that many people, inside and outside the business community, believe that it is really not possible to earn an honest living, or to meet one's expenses without serious compromise of moral principles like honesty, social responsibility and fair dealing. But as we proceed with this discussion, hopefully we'll see why and how good ethical practices amount to good business, although this realization isn't likely to follow immediately.

Q. 2. What do we really *mean* by the expression "business ethics"?

We should begin by defining our terms, at least in a preliminary way, although hopefully a fuller understanding will come later. The traditional exercise in "definition of terms" involves isolating each term in an expression or phrase and analyzing it separately, so as to come to an understanding of the entire concept. So perhaps the question should be in two parts: What do we mean by "business" and what do we mean by "ethics"? The second of these terms is certainly going to be more complex, but that doesn't mean we don't need to look at the first in some detail. *Let us first analyze the word "business," with "ethics" to come later.*

We tend to make great use of the expression "business" in our society: "Mind your own *business*," "It's none of my *business*," "Let's get down to *business*," and so forth. And, of course, we talk about doing things in a "businesslike" manner, which brings us much closer to what I have in mind. In this context, when we use the term "business" we mean *the exchange of goods and services in some relationship of contractual obligation,* or what some people prefer to call "commerce." This can also be expressed in terms of the *basic legal ingredients of a contract: 1) mutual consent* (orally, in writing or implied by the acts of the parties, depending on a variety of circumstances and sometimes governed by statute), *2) capacity of the parties* (they are sane and of legal age for consent), and *3) consideration* (the exchange of goods and services having value), in addition to the requisite element that a contract, to be binding and enforceable legally, must have *4) a "lawful object,"* meaning that it does not ask anyone to do something which is either impossible or against the law. I think you will find that, even informally or implicitly, these factors are present in all business relationships and activities.

Q. 3. Is the term "business" limited to those activities that are designed or intended to make money, or a profit?

No. There are many "not for profit" enterprises that need to be run "like a business" or else they will never achieve their goals. Churches, homeless shelters, soup kitchens and a host of other endeavors exist to serve human need out of religious or charitable motives, as distinct from the ever popular and well publicized profit motive. As a result, in recent years we have tended to think of figures like Mother Teresa as being in a totally different area of human life from the well known and celebrated "moguls," "tycoons" and "captains of industry." But if someone doesn't "take care of business" in a charitable or philanthropic organization or endeavor, then the insurance and legal requirements won't be met, the food won't be served in accord with legitimate health regulations, and so forth. Also—since volunteers alone can't run most of these operations—employees will need to be hired and compensated in keeping with the laws that surround the organization in the larger society. Even in religious orders, including monasteries of cloistered monks and nuns, someone has to take care of managing the property, feeding the members of the community, taking care of the legal and financial needs of those who become sick, and documenting the choices made by those who opt to take vows of poverty, for these things have ramifications in terms of property rights and legal consent.

By way of extension, we can include in our discussion those areas of economic activity commonly referred to as "professions," like medicine, law, education and so on. Even though these walks of life tend to be described by the lofty term of "profession" (implying specialized training, education and dedication to public service) as distinct from business, they all have their "business aspects" and in addition tend to develop "professional ethics." We'll discuss some examples along those lines as we go on, but the point to remember for now is that your neighborhood physician, schoolteacher, dentist or minister of religion is in some sense a businessperson with a concern for business or professional ethics as part of his or her dedication to public service and obligations to the community in general as well as to a particular clientele being served.

Q. 4. Are even religious, charitable and philanthropic organizations, in a sense, "businesses," and therefore bound to certain standards of business or professional ethics?

Yes, and one of the main concerns in our society today—if you listen to the discussion programs that are broadcast or read some of the thought-provoking articles that are published in newspapers and magazines—is professional ethics, in a variety of areas, to the extent that people feel something is quite wrong, that some kind of social contract has been violated, and that innocent people have in some way been wronged or cheated. These reflect a departure from professional ethics, even if we are not always sure of just what professional ethics should be or call for in every case. But to say more about that right now is to get ahead of the discussion. *We need first to define the second part of that expression, "business ethics."*

Q. 5. Aren't morality and ethics pretty much the same?

The lines of demarcation do tend to be a little fuzzy. As Mr. Cook said in the address I mentioned earlier:

> How do we define ethical conduct? One view is that anything which is legal is ethical—legal standards are appropriate standards to measure ethical conduct. At the opposite extreme, the view is that anytime you're in doubt, anytime your conscience gnaws at you, you're probably engaging in unethical conduct. I think the true standard is somewhere in between (*ibid.*).

Cook reflects the views of a great many people, I think, to the effect that there is some distinction between the terms involved, although the distinction is not an easy one to make. Here's the way I see it.

Morality—beliefs about the rightness or wrongness of human acts—would be what people understand as a matter of conscience, coming from our values as shaped in families, communities and religious bodies. Without trying to be pedantic, I should note here that the word "conscience" comes from Latin roots, meaning literally "to know *with* [emphasis mine]"; in other words, an individual's conscience is really a manifestation of the influence of some sort of group conscience. For instance, some people—because of family, community or religious influences—believe some acts to be wrong by their nature (sexual intimacy outside marriage, blood transfusions, smoking, gambling, abortion, drinking alcohol) whereas others do not. Without going into the specific discipline of moral theology in a detailed way, it could be said that how a religious tradition views the nature of humanity and certain aspects of life (the dignity and proper care of the human body, the meaning of sexual imagery and the institution of marriage, the value of human life and when it begins), in the context of a religious point of view or revelation, will lead to certain moral conclusions about particular human acts.

Ethics usually involves standards of practice or categories of acceptable and unacceptable behavior agreed upon by a group with shared interests, for the sake of achieving those interests. For instance, the medical profession has for centuries dealt with ethical standards they believe to be for the benefit of both the doctor and the patient. One of these is the doctrine of *non nocere,* meaning the obligation "to do no harm." The practical application of this means that when a physician cannot likely heal a patient, at least nothing should be done which is risky to the point of doing harm. As we shall discuss later, other professions also have their own internal ethical codes. Some of the occupations involved include stockbrokers, attorneys, college admissions officers, real estate agents, teachers and journalists, to make brief mention of only a few examples.

Q. 6. Isn't there some "overlap" between morality and ethics, as in expressions like the Judaeo-Christian, or more specifically the Protestant "ethic"?

In that sense, yes. To use the example just mentioned, we can say that there is a certain set of beliefs concerning appropriate conduct which, by common consensus, seems to pertain to everyone who has been influenced by the religious values and outlooks of Protestantism, at least in North America and probably most of Europe—and this would include many Jews, Roman Catholics and other people who are not Protestant church members!

We tend to think of this ethical viewpoint as putting high value on hard work done honestly, deferred gratification as a way of avoiding a series of weaknesses and crippling debts and other dependencies, self-sufficiency in combination with helping those in need, and a series of other virtues which are influenced by a definite point of view.

By way of further explanation, I recall a homily I once heard in a Sunday liturgy at the Jesuit institution where I studied and now teach. The priest—a philosophy professor—gave a fine talk about what he called "ethics" based on the teachings of the gospel. Despite the excellence of his content, I would have quarreled with his terminology, and argued that what he really talked about was not so much *ethics* as *Christian morality*. On the other hand, it could be said that there is certainly such a thing as a "Christian ethic" subscribed to by those who follow the doctrines of Jesus either in general or as communicated by a particular church, in this instance Roman Catholic (where the conscience is informed by the teachings of the popes and councils of the church). So, in that sense, it is to be expected that the terms "morality" and "ethics" might be used almost interchangeably by people who share a religious vision of what constitutes appropriate and inappropriate behaviors.

It should be remembered, though, that many people in the business community share ethically in a decision making process, again concerning appropriate and inappropriate behaviors, *without* any direct influence from any religious vision or tradition. At most, there are the individual religious and moral values of the persons making up the business community in a given situation. But the background for ethical decisions will not be any sort of personal moral conviction or religious creed. It will be, simply, what the members of a consensual group working together for a business objective decide together will be acceptable or unacceptable conduct. These sorts of decisions will be made on the basis of what are essentially business values, and the influence of any moral or religious values may be at most coincidental. However, there may be considerable strength in terms of the indirect or "background" influence of such values as they form a good part of the overall vision and expectations of the community surrounding the business decision.

Q. 7. Many people, often from a moral or ethical point of view, tend to use expressions like "There ought to be a law!" Where does legality fit in here?

Legality—much to the dismay of some who hold strong religious views about moral issues—often has little or nothing to do with morality. For that matter, it often has little or nothing to do with what most of us would consider fair. A famous law professor at Rutgers University in New Jersey once said, "The words *fair* and *unfair* have no meaning in a court of law!" His intention was not to scoff at fairness or encourage its opposite, but simply to point out the dispassionate impartiality of the legal system as a reflection of society, from which we get the famous image of the statue of justice wearing a blindfold. We have all heard the saying "Life is not fair," and laws are meant to regulate life, not to change it.

Civil law specifies what society will and will not tolerate, in a system designed not necessarily to make life beautiful or people good but to avoid chaos.

For instance, society tries to prevent intoxicated drivers from getting behind the wheel, but needs to define what constitutes intoxication. On the other hand, society does not prohibit the production, possession, sale or consumption of alcoholic beverages, except in certain circumstances that are viewed as dangerous to society as a whole (sale of alcoholic beverages made without supervision and proper labeling, sale to minors or intoxicated persons, etc.). In the United States, when the Volstead Act attempted to impose the convictions of "prohibitionists" upon the rest of American society, the law was a failure and was repealed. Now, in most states at least, we have laws which only govern but do not totally prohibit the use of alcoholic beverages. No doubt, there are many people in charge of administering these laws who would be happier if no one produced, sold or consumed alcoholic beverages at all, but the law is simply saying that if people are going to do this, they must do it in a way which is not harmful to other members of society. It seems this is a case of a less extreme form of governmental supervision that people can live with when a more extreme form has been tried and found wanting, and when no one wants an atmosphere of anarchy with no supervision and regulation at all in this area.

Q. 8. Should civil societies never attempt to pass laws that reflect moral vision?

Perhaps it's *never* a good idea to say "never." But we do well to remember the lessons learned with prohibition, which we just mentioned. The difficulty with laws like the Volstead Act is that they are what I call "laws of public outrage." What really takes place here is that the majority of the society uses law to show how much they are offended by a particular behavior, in this case the consumption of alcoholic beverages. But the question needs to be asked: "*How,* specifically, will this law help to keep order and prevent chaos in our society?" When prohibition failed, it was because the law was almost impossible to enforce: those who took exception to it found that their violations were hard to detect, and that a variety of persons—including public officials charged with enforcement of the law—found monetary incentives to flout the law. The same has tended to be true of a variety of other "public outrage" laws. Sadly, it often occurs that folks muster the political strength to "outlaw," or thus seemingly prevent, a type of behavior they find repugnant, but it becomes impossible to actually stop people from engaging in that behavior when they are determined to do so; in some cases it actually happens that there is some increase in the behavior in question, often with considerable—maybe even unacceptable—social cost attending the effort at enforcing the prohibition. In some cases this might be the old "forbidden fruit" theory at work: you know, outlaw a type of behavior that some people find attractive, and others who had not engaged in it will wonder what they were missing all along. In some other cases it might be that the prohibited activity increases because people are angry at its being forbidden.

Q. 9. Should a society avoid making unenforceable laws, or increase the police power of society to better enforce existing laws?

A massive enforcement effort can make almost any law appear to work, at least on the surface, simply because the forces amassed by society to enforce it make violation of the law so costly or painful that very few people will take lightly the risk of being caught breaking the law. A good example—without getting bogged down in the details of the case—might be the alleged "graffiti" vandalization of automobiles by some young men, including an American, in Singapore back in 1994. When the American was "caned," this was in keeping with the severe codes of Singapore and the incident drew attention to the fact that Singapore, with its tight enforcement, has very few violations of such laws. On the other hand, it could be said that the reason why the laws are enforced so strictly is that Singaporeans as a group have arrived at a consensus in favor of such laws. By way of contrast, there are cities in the United States where public opinion considers the enforcement of some laws—though these are actually on the statute books—to be of relatively low priority, such as the prohibition of prostitution or possession of certain controlled substances, as well as "graffiti." There are even some places where the citizens or their elected representatives have voted to not enforce some laws at all, as in San Francisco where the Board of Supervisors has declared the city and county a "sanctuary" free of enforcement of laws against illegal immigrants, or certain parts of California where the sheriff or police department has been instructed not to enforce laws against possession of marijuana.

It has even happened that a referendum on the ballot, withholding services like public education and health care to undocumented aliens, has found its way to success at the polls, in California's 1994 measure [Proposition #187], but the enforcement of the law was stalled by the courts on constitutional grounds. Even those who take the position that the law could be constitutional have been heard to wonder how it would ever be enforced in a practical way.

The point I am making by the above examples is that you can enforce the law strictly by external means, but it will not be successful over the long term unless something has been done to bring about an interior disposition on the part of the people which is in sympathy with the spirit of the law. The Greek of the New Testament used the word *metanoia* to signify an interior "change of heart" as the sort of goal Jesus was striving for in his teaching, as contrasted with the external legalism he criticized in the Pharisees and scribes. This doesn't mean that those much-maligned rabbis, who sincerely loved the law that had come to them through centuries of Jewish tradition, were nothing more than cold-hearted and superficial people, but simply that exterior law without interiorization of the law ultimately leads to disregard of the law. Think of someone driving at one mile per hour under the speed limit simply because a police officer is watching, but who then drives like a lunatic when the police car goes away. What does that do for safety on the road, unless you have eight police cars per square mile patrolling twenty-four hours a day? Somehow you have to arrive at a consensus in favor of "doing the right thing," whatever the right thing happens to be in a given situation, in order to ensure a reasonable probability that the right thing will be done.

Q. 10. Is there such a thing as a universal, trans-cultural set of values, or not?

In an age when there is a strong emphasis on respect for cultural diversity, many people would be inclined to say, "No, there really is not a universal set of moral values!" However, I wonder if it is really as simple as that.

While it is true that not all religions and philosophies will exhibit the exact teachings of Christianity in detail, for instance, I think that they all demonstrate a concern for values which we would identify as "honesty," "decency," or what I have referred to above as "doing the right thing."

On the one hand, we find that Muslims and Christians, for instance, differ when it comes to certain values like monogamy in marriage. We also find that not all religious belief systems embrace the Hindu ideal of non-violence or demonstrate as well as Taoists do the notion of respect for nature and balance in the universe.

On the other hand, we find common areas in general: respect for marriage and the family (whether in a monogamous or polygamous context), abhorrence for gratuitous violence (questions of self-defense or "holy war" aside), and a concern for the environment (though western religions appear to be latecomers to this party). This means that we do well to speak from our cultures and traditions about moral and ethical concerns, because in so doing we illuminate our own consciences and share them with others. I realize it is much more difficult to engage in persuasive dialogue than to simply say, "This is the moral law in the case because the pope (or Muhammad or Moses or whoever) said so!" But that is the reality of the situation. For this reason I will not be hesitant to refer to the scriptures of Christianity and its antecedent Old Testament, as well as to the teachings of the popes and the World Council of Churches, when I feel that they generate more light than heat. On the other hand, I hardly expect such utterances to settle all questions in all minds, forever, without any "feedback."

It is my hope, though, that by engaging in the sort of dialogue I have just mentioned, people who are willing to spend the time and energy required will emerge with respect not only for each other as persons but also for the religious and moral insights which come from the hearts of us all, and which I feel call upon us to be better than we are, to take human life to a higher plane than what we are accustomed to from the nightly newscasts and headlines, and help us lead ourselves and others to a vision which—whether or not specifically Christian or Jewish or Shinto—is certainly more human in the truest, fullest sense of that term.

Q. 11. How does development of moral consciousness in a diverse society work?

When members of the business community, or society at large, feel that certain kinds of actions are fair or unfair, beneficial or detrimental, they usually draw from some common or prevalent ideas about morality as applied to certain actions. The ethical canons in most professions, which abhor fraud and urge full and fair disclosure of material facts, are different in their scope of authority from the religious saying, "It's a sin to tell a lie," but both express the same belief and have similar results. Moreover, the various governments of our societies around the world all recognize that unfair dealing, fraud and deceit generate chaos, and laws are passed and enforced accordingly, even though the specific aspects of the various ordinances will differ from time to time and place to place, with a myriad of applications to various circumstances.

Q. 12. Are people in business really *interested* in being either ethical or moral, or following the law?

Some obviously don't care, as long as they don't get *caught* breaking the law. I realize, at once, that this sounds very cynical and hardly reflects an optimistic view concerning human nature. However, if these people make decisions which result in actions that hurt others, this kind of thing eventually tends to come to light, and public confidence in them or in their company is hurt, sometimes quite seriously. That consequence is more damaging, usually, than having to pay a fine for violating some statute, especially in an age when business seems to operate under the glare of spotlights and the gaze of microscopes. For this sort of reason, more businesses than ever before are concerned with doing business "ethically," whatever that turns out to mean.

Q. 13. Is it correct to assume that "business ethics" has not always been this important, or that the emphasis on it is new?

In a sense, concerns of business ethics have always been with us, of course. But there really has been a greatly heightened awareness of business ethics in recent years. There is at least one prestigious journal on the national scene dedicated specifically to the study of business ethics (the *Journal of Business Ethics*). There are meetings in corporations and in academic and religious circles alike to study business ethics (for instance, the Society for Christian Ethics). There are numerous articles in popular magazines and newspapers concerning business ethics. This subject is a frequent topic on panel discussions and "talk shows" on radio and TV, as well as in public lectures at prestigious venues such as public forums, libraries, civic associations and the like. Many colleges and universities offer business ethics courses, either in the humanities departments like philosophy and religion, or in the business schools—sometimes both, despite the widespread caution that ethics cannot really be "taught" in the same sense that straight-line depreciation can. Often, in undergraduate and MBA programs in schools of business, the curriculum in ethics takes place under the wing of the course area known as organizational behavior or "O.B."—sometimes as a subset of the discipline of "management." It's difficult, nowadays, to have a conversation of any length with people involved in the study of the humanities without some mention of business ethics, and even more difficult to avoid that topic when communicating with those who are engaged in the study and practice of contemporary business.

Part II

THE IMPORT AND IMPACT OF BUSINESS ETHICS TODAY

Q. 14. How was the atmosphere for business ethics different in the past?

Consumers are different today from what they were even a generation ago. There was a time when the average person was relatively unsophisticated as to how products and services were delivered, and what their legal rights to redress would be if a product or service turned out to be unsatisfactory. At the same time, the level of economic activity tended to be more small-time. Folks bought from neighbors or through distributors in their own communities, so there tended to be a built-in level of immediate accountability in terms of dealing with local merchants, such as the neighborhood grocer, service station or pharmacist—you know, the old-fashioned "corner store" idea. Perhaps it could be observed that, even in the days when the typical consumer didn't have a complex structure for redress, he or she didn't really need it that much anyway. In the past, at least in most of the United States, businesses which were still "getting off the ground" were in the early stages of building their reputations; they were very dependent on consumer satisfaction and did a great deal to lend credibility to the "brand names" they represented. On the other side of that coin, customers tended to be very loyal to those brands, once they felt that they had been treated fairly and got real value for their money. We have all heard of "old-timers" who would only buy one brand of automobile from one specific dealer and put only one brand of gasoline in it, getting their service at the same local station. Such folks tended to go to the same grocery store all the time, buying only one brand of soap and drinking only one brand of beer or soft drink. In a word, business ethics tended to be important years ago too, in terms of building reputations with individuals in communities, but things got taken care of closer to home, or with more immediacy at or near what marketing folks call the "point of sale." Our ancestors tended to believe that they could trust the people with whom they did business, or else they would find someone else to trade with in a hurry, and let all their friends and neighbors in on the kinds of decisions they made about such matters.

Q. 15. How and why is the marketplace different today?

The accountability factor is different, the contact is more remote, and at the same time the stakes are higher.

The way companies are bought and sold these days, a movie studio can own a textbook publishing company and a newspaper can own a baseball team or a cigarette manufacturer can own a soft drink bottler; a fire insurance company can own—or be owned by—a company that produces convenience foods, and so on.

Today, consumers tend to be more removed from the ultimate level of accountability. Misunderstandings and communication breakdowns occur; people tend to feel alienated; manufacturers often misread the public need. In this sort of atmosphere, a company can hardly afford to be thought of as "unethical" in dealing with its clientele, especially when some important brand names are marketed all over the world. At the same time, many businesses operate in a litigious atmosphere, where lawsuits abound, especially when significant numbers of people feel they have been injured in the same way and they can spread out their legal costs in a "class action suit." Often, a corporation tries to "put out the fire" and exercise "damage control," sometimes in ways that are counter-productive when they appear to be "stonewalling" people or "covering up" in an embarrassing situation. When that sort of thing looks as if it is about to happen, it often attracts the attention of "action line," "consumer protection" or other kinds of services sponsored by newspapers or broadcast stations—or even the sort of exposé programs that appear on the national TV networks.

In summing up, I guess you could say the need for, and the considerations of, business ethics have become more sophisticated and more complicated.

Q. 16. Has "business ethics" really become more important today, then?

If it hasn't become more important, it's certainly receiving more emphasis, which practically amounts to the same thing. This seems true, especially as we move into an age of greater consumer awareness and public protection. People today feel they work so hard for their money that they want to be taken care of if they're not happy with the goods and services they buy. On the other hand, people who work providing goods and services want to be treated ethically by their employers; they want a day's fair wage for a day's fair work, just as their employers want the converse. Finally, men and women in business don't want their competitors to have unfair advantages over them as a result of some kind of unethical behavior. We all know how we would feel if we worked hard in preparing a paper or exam in school and got a "C+" or a "B-" and found that one of our classmates had received an "A" as the result of plagiarism or cheating in some form. The same kind of thing is a concern in the business world, often with stakes that people think of as being higher than those in the school example I just gave, although the basic feeling of "Damn it, it's not fair!" is still at the root of it all.

Q. 17. Have corporations really become *convinced*, in any genuine, internalized way, that there is truly a need for doing business more ethically, or—again—is it really a public relations ploy with a desire to not get caught?

That's hard to say. Different corporate cultures obviously operate with different visions and values. However, it could be said that if the result is ethical behavior, the motive is almost secondary, at least from the standpoint of society as a whole.

Q. 18. Isn't it flippant or cynical to emphasize results—in a sort of pragmatic way—without stressing interior motive or attitude?

Not really. It's more realistic than supposing that noble ethical principles can be cultivated, in somewhat of a vacuum, in the hearts and minds of everyone in the business community. Let's face it: from the classic standpoint of traditional Catholic theology (to use a frame of reference that may be familiar to many), more people seem to express imperfect contrition (fear of eternal punishment) than perfect contrition (sorrow over offending a loving God). Sometimes an awareness of what can happen to people when they do wrong is more immediately convincing than a philosophically or theologically sophisticated appreciation of how a perfect moral system should operate. Besides, public consciousness of ethical values tends to change from time to time, and business reacts to that. In that sense, it can be said that a basic principle is being followed, namely that of listening—in many senses of that term—to the customers, finding out what they want and attempting to provide it. As I've suggested before, this is just plain "good business," regardless of any loftier motives that may or may not also attend the situation. Ethical conduct for less than angelic motives may be short of the mark in the vision of idealists, but it has a tangible beneficial result for the meantime in the practical order, and it is certainly a result that most people I know would be more than willing to settle for until something better comes along.

Q. 19. What are examples of business adapting to changing public attitudes on ethics?

In addition to consumer awareness, mentioned previously, there's a tendency for many people in the economy to resort to what I call "the guerrilla warfare of the pocketbook." Some like to reward or penalize companies for engaging in certain kinds of behavior that have nothing to do with the product or service being delivered. For example, many folks began years ago to boycott a certain beer since they felt the brewery discriminated against minorities in hiring. It had nothing to do with how the beer tasted. Another example, over the years, has involved the many people who have refused to buy lettuce or table grapes not picked by union farmworkers.

In yet another case with special poignance in one major city, a department store hired a number of Catholic high school boys to help them with the Christmas rush; they agreed that the monies they earned would go to the school's fund drive. The store, saying it was in the midst of financial difficulties, paid its regular employees (who, after all, were protected by union contracts) but told the boys they would have to wait. Months, and eventually a couple of years, went by; the boys and their school received no money, while the store filed for bankruptcy. When the public in that area became aware of what happened, a number of donors made up the amount to the school fund drive but, more importantly, large numbers of people began to boycott the store, writing letters to the management to let them know that this action was being taken because the boys had not been paid as they had been promised they would be.

In the kinds of situations we have just considered, it may well be that the internal process of the producer is given more significance than the product itself, in terms of how members of the public view the ethical behavior (or lack of same) of the company in question.

Q. 20. When public pressure can be brought to bear, what are people in business generally doing, or how are they responding?

There's no one standard response. Some businesses, depending on their nature and market position, are essentially saying, "We can't let outside pressures dictate how we run our shop." And sometimes they may be right. On the other hand, many more businesses seem to be saying, "Let's do a better job of cultivating goodwill with the public." It's in that sort of atmosphere that many decisions get made that are more ethical, or at least more ethically sensitive, than the kinds of decisions that might have been made fifty, or even twenty, years ago. There is a much more acute sense of "being watched" in the business community as a segment of the overall society at large.

Part III

ETHICS WITHIN PROFESSIONS—
A NEW CONSCIOUSNESS

Q. 21. Would that be true even in the so-called "professions" with their supposedly high motives of public service and the idea of their being somehow "above" the world of business?

Most definitely. The accountability level of various professions has increased dramatically in recent years. This can serve to illustrate what we discussed previously, about how every profession or enterprise, however elevated or philanthropic, is in effect a business subject to the rules and expectations of ethical behavior governing business in general.

Q. 22. Why has this sort of change taken place in the professions today?

I believe this kind of change is due to several factors. One reason for this is that such professions as medicine, education, the clergy and law tended in the past to assume that the members of these professions themselves knew what was best for the people they served, without receiving a significant amount of input (and sometimes none at all) from those people. This occurred, often, because the members of the professions in question were often the only members of society who were educated and articulate enough to conceptualize and express standards of professional ethics. The goal of "universal literacy" has been within sight only in the last couple of centuries, in many of the developed countries, and now electronic and visual communication are such that literacy is no longer considered an essential requisite of participation in public discourse—just look at the "talk shows" on radio and TV. Until recently, the average citizen in most places felt genuinely unqualified—and, to be honest, downright afraid—to express any opinion at all about what sort of service should be forthcoming from "professional people," who by virtue of their educations and appropriate certifications were presumed to know what their responsibilities and obligations were.

Also, in the societies of past centuries, including the bulk of the century now ending, there was a presumption of a hierarchical sort of structure in which the better-educated (and, typically, also more affluent) members of society were entitled to more of a voice—both officially and in a variety of unofficial ways—in what went on and what was acceptable in everyday life. Remember, when the United States was in its infancy as a "democracy," as recently as two centuries ago, only property owners were allowed to vote, and the ranks of the electorate routinely excluded such minorities as non-Caucasians and non-Protestants, to say nothing of women. These things have changed only gradually, mostly because of changes in law resulting from public awareness and social activism, coming to a point of real transition only within the last thirty or so years. As a consequence, people without either wealth or education (in other words, those outside "the professions") tended to be thought of as having "no right to talk back" in virtually any area of life.

But the changes over the twentieth century, in countries all over the world, will make the twenty-first century vastly different from the nineteenth. The former colonies of the British empire are now independent in one sense or another. The former colonies of European countries in Africa and South America are now sovereign nations. The supposed monolithic structure of the Soviet Union and its satellites has broken up. Even China, long recognized as a tightly controlled society under emperors and communists alike, seems to be affording its individual citizens more freedom than before. So we are now beginning a new century in which more and more individuals feel they have a voice and the will to use it, whether or not the place in which they live conforms to a strict definition of a free society or a participatory democracy.

What all this amounts to, concerning the perception of "professional ethics," is that the people who are served by the members of the professions are much more likely than before to make their voices heard.

None of this is meant as taking away from the preparation and expertise of the professional men and women who serve the society around them. Nor is it meant to say that the patient knows better than the doctor or the student knows better than the professor. What I'm striving to point out here is a change in the tone of the relationship, wherein the consumers of professional services are much more likely than before to be interactive, rather than passive.

Q. 23. But how will this affect, or how does it now affect, professional ethics?

In my view, this sort of social "sea change" is affecting the basic "rules of engagement" so that standards for professional ethics will come from the consumer's relationship to the profession and not simply from within the profession itself. To illustrate, at one time both attorneys and physicians had determined, within their respective professional associations (American Bar Association and American Medical Association), that it was unethical for them to advertise their services to the general public. There was no evidence to suggest that there would be anything immoral in their advertising, and apparently no law to prohibit them from doing it. It's just that the barristers and doctors considered advertising themselves to be sort of unseemly or "beneath their dignity." It also seemed to smack of competition within the ranks, in an atmosphere which presumed that clients or patients came to the office on the basis of a referral or because of professional reputation or visibility (in some cases simply a well-located office) within a locality. No one, in those days, wanted to appear to be "poaching" upon the clients or patients of another member of the professional "fraternity."

As time went on, some interesting changes developed. One was that there were more and more lawyers and doctors in proportion to the general public in many areas, wishing to serve the same potential clientele. This was especially true in urban centers, where an increasing number of professionals, to say nothing of the populace as a whole, were strangers to the community and had no "referral network." The public wanted to know which professionals were available and what they had to offer. The lawyers and doctors wanted to make known their particular areas of expertise and service. So, in time, the professional ethics concerning advertising underwent a change, by the consent of the members of the profession.

Q. 24. As you admit, that's an example of something without either moral or legal significance. But what about something that *does* have moral or legal significance?

Perhaps the most vivid example—and the most controversial—would involve abortion. According to the professional ethics of medicine for centuries, abortion was prohibited by the Oath of Hippocrates, which has traditionally been recited by graduates of medical schools and framed on the walls of many physicians' offices. This part of the Hippocratic Oath arose from the moral belief (which was held before Christianity) that abortion was murder. As time went on, an increasing number of physicians came to believe that abortion could be justified morally, at least in some circumstances; this was a matter which they had decided on in their own consciences, but abortion was still prohibited by the ethics of their profession. In addition, abortion was against the law in many societies around the world, including the United States. But when the U.S. Supreme Court, in 1973, held in the case of *Roe v. Wade* that choosing an abortion was the legal right of a woman, the professional ethics of abortion were reconsidered, so that doctors (and others such as nurses) may perform or assist in abortions. Many refuse to do so, because it violates their own moral consciences, even if civil law and professional ethics now permit this activity. Their conviction (like my own) is that if something is inherently wrong, a law or a canon of professional ethics cannot make it right. But this is a good example of how ethics, morality and law do not always come to compatible conclusions. As a result, agonized debate on this kind of subject will certainly continue.

Q. 25. Abortion is, of course, an issue that "makes headlines," and the divisions are clear on this subject. Are there other examples of professional ethical standards that are perhaps more subtle?

Here it may be helpful to consider professional standards which go beyond the prohibitions required by civil law, to make sure that even the hint of illegality or unfair dealing will be avoided, so as to safeguard the good name of the profession and its members as a whole. Some of these involve taking additional precautions to make sure that no one will accuse a member of the profession of having committed any sort of impropriety.

As an experienced educator on both the secondary and university levels, I have in mind the standards for professional conduct utilized by private school and college admissions officers, which would not be known to the general public. Without going into excessive detail, these rules are meant to avoid any institution having an unfair advantage in recruiting desirable students. The regulations are not a matter of law, but reflect a sense of fairness on the part of those who work in the admissions divisions of numerous educational institutions. For example, the payment to agents of finder's fees for students to enroll in some private prep schools was a subject of recent ethical controversy, as reported by the *Wall Street Journal:*

> Taking such fees violates an ethics code for placement counselors in the U.S. "Schools should not be the client; the client should be the family," says Virginia deVeer, admissions director at Tabor Academy in Marion, Mass. "If I'm paying an agency to find me three kids from Spain, that agency won't have the kids' interest in mind, it'll have my interest" ("The New Preppies," Vol. CXXX, No. 39, February 25, 1994, pg. A7).

In the same article it is said that "Paying agents finder's fees for students is criticized by some schools, and an embarrassment to others that engage in the practice" (*ibid.*). And one admissions director "says he is troubled by the fact that he paid $1,650 to Korean agents for each of the seven Korean students at the school. 'I'm not too excited about admitting it,' he says. 'I'd like to be able not to use them. On the other hand, they do supply us with good students'" (*ibid.*).

Another instance arose some years ago concerning reporters covering sporting events, specifically major league baseball. Influenced to no small degree by the code of ethics of the Society of Professional Journalists, various newspapers became uncomfortable with the idea of their writers accepting flights on team charters, or meals in lunchrooms operated for the press by the baseball teams, even though there was no other practical way to cover games or to obtain a meal and take a necessary break, quickly and privately, during a long day of interviewing and game coverage. The Society's Code of Ethics, Section III, Part 1, says:

Journalists must be free of obligation to any interest other than the public's right to know the truth.

1. Gifts, favors, free travel, special treatment or privileges can compromise the integrity of journalists and their employers. Nothing of value should be accepted (*The Quill*, Vol. 79, No. 9, November/December, 1991, pg. 23).

Eventually a popular solution, beginning in the early 1990s, was that the travel arrangements and meals would still be provided, as a matter of convenience, but with the correspondents or their employers paying for them at market rates, so that there is no hint of any undue influence which could taint the reporter's coverage.

In the real estate profession, the National Association of Realtors (a voluntary trade organization) had an article in its code of ethics which forbade a broker who was a Realtor from soliciting the services of a sales agent working under another Realtor; this practice was considered a form of "poaching" that was unethical—if not tantamount to interference with a contractual relationship and thereby legally actionable—and which brought about disharmony between Realtors. At the NAR convention at San Francisco in 1982 it was decided that it made sense to delete this prohibition, providing the soliciting Realtor afforded the employing competitor the courtesy of a notice about the contemplated recruitment offer (NAR Code of Ethics, Article 22).

Q. 26. Those kinds of things sound like "housekeeping" and, to a large degree, "damage control," to avoid conflict between members of a given professional group or to avoid charges of wrongdoing from outside. Doesn't it get any better than this?

I hope so. Again referring to the Society of Professional Journalists, their code is a model of canons for fair treatment of the subjects of reporting, while at the same time defensive of the reading public's right to know (*loc. cit.*, Sections IV and V). There are definite and specific regulations designed to ensure the objectivity of the reporter and the even-handed coverage of a story which may be controversial as regards either the person(s) or the subject matter in question. Or concerning the Realtors again, their code is designed to ensure compliance with civil law and public expectation in a variety of areas such as fair housing, full and fair disclosure, and so on (NAR Code, *passim*; cf. Code of Ethics and Professional Conduct, Department of Real Estate, State of California, Commissioner's Regulations #s 2785ff). As a matter of fact, the NAR code refers to many of its sections as "aspirational," meaning that without any concrete problem at hand they are intended to elevate the overall standards of behavior and service in the profession.

Q. 27. Does this kind of professional consciousness of ethics always have to take the form of a code coming from a specific professional society?

Of course not. As a long-time teacher on various levels, I can tell you that teachers as a group have developed a sense of what is ethically acceptable or unacceptable even though many have never belonged to a specific group that promulgates a particular code of ethics. For instance, teachers generally agree that it is inappropriate to accept gifts from students, since these might be construed as inducements to favor in a system which should be built upon objective grading. On the other hand, it is recognized that objective grading cannot ignore legitimate personal needs, like those of the student with dyslexia who cannot distinguish "b" from "d" on a multiple choice exam. In fact, to refuse to provide an alternative measurement instrument for such a student, properly identified, would in itself be considered a form of unfairness. These are things that teachers simply know, or learn as they go along and face concrete situations.

Q. 28. Doesn't that mean that codes or standards of professional ethics—not just for teachers but for doctors and lawyers and others—have to be updated constantly, as new questions and issues come to the fore?

Definitely. Here we can look again at the medical and legal professions. Years ago the idea of a physician or attorney having a sexual relationship with a patient or client was virtually unheard of. Most people, inside and outside of these professions, would have never thought of such a thing and, if they did, they would have considered it a way of taking unfair advantage of one's position of authority and influence in dealing with a person who is likely to be, if not awestruck, at least dependent or vulnerable. Nowadays, there are numerous cases of doctors and lawyers who have had sexual relationships with people who have come to their offices for professional services. Sometimes this sort of thing becomes the object of public scandal in the newspapers, often because the patients or clients complain after the fact that they were taken advantage of in a situation where they felt powerless. In the old days, when most members of the medical and legal professions were far more likely to be guided by stringent Judaeo-Christian views concerning sexual behavior, and when discussions of private conduct were more circumspect, such controversies would not have arisen as they have in modern times. As a result, the ABA and AMA have been giving serious consideration to the circumstances under which sexual activity with a client or patient is considered appropriate or inappropriate, and the process of shaping those ethical standards is still ongoing.

Q. 29. Medicine and law, like education, are professions in which the practitioner is often thought of as "playing God." But nowhere is that more likely to be an issue than among members of the clergy. Are there developing standards of professional conduct or ethics for the clergy?

Yes, although as in other cases there is some blurring between "morality" and "ethics." I point this out because, on the one hand, the moral vision of a religious belief system should obviously be the benchmark by which that religion's ministers (although they are human beings like everyone else) conduct themselves, with a view to the highest moral standards for behavior, fidelity to the teachings of their religion and dedication to the good of those dependent upon them for spiritual and moral leadership. But, on the other hand, some religions have few or no specific moral guidelines that would govern the clergy's relationships to the members of the congregation, and it has even been shown in some "cult" religions that the structure is set up so as to allow the "religious leaders" to exploit their congregants physically, sexually and financially—"the shepherd fleecing the flock," so to speak. It has also occurred, even in some religions that have strong teachings about honesty, money, sexual propriety and other matters, that some members of the clergy have diverged from the path laid out for them by the teachings of their religious body. When this takes place, regardless of the motivations or limitations of the ministers in question, members of the congregation often are shocked and become irate, frequently to the point of suing the members of the clergy involved, demanding their removal from service, or both. In addition, some disillusioned worshipers leave the churches they were raised in and felt they could depend upon. It is their way of saying that they expect their clergy to be accountable.

Part IV

ETHICS IN THE MARKETPLACE—
BUYING AND SELLING;
FRAUD AND INSIDER TRADING

Q. 30. Would it be fair to say, in a nutshell, that people who depend on and support the doctors, real estate agents, lawyers, teachers or members of any other profession, including the clergy, are becoming a good deal more active and self-protective as consumers, as part of the overall atmosphere of contemporary society?

Yes. People are much more concerned today than ever before about getting what they feel they have a right to, in terms of either what they have paid for or been led to expect or depend upon. This has translated into a large number of people using their own intelligence and industry to do for themselves some of the tasks they used to entrust to professionals, as in the "For Sale by Owner [FSBO]" phenomenon in real estate or the "In Pro Per" self-help law movement. Even when such individuals do, in fact, contract with the appropriate professionals, they do so with a more critical eye as to the services they will receive and the prices they will pay. The overall result is educated consumerism, whether or not it shows itself in a "do-it-yourself" mode.

Q. 31. Does this relate to a changing attitude on the old doctrine of "let the buyer beware"?

Sure! That old principle, commonly known by the Latin phrase *Caveat emptor* in the legal profession, meant that the buyer had virtually all the responsibility in a purchase transaction. This view is not accurate today, if it ever really was.

In the old days, if the goods or services paid for were deficient, then the unhappy buyer was presumed to have made the mistake of not looking out for himself or herself to a sufficient degree. Today, though, the tendency is toward "consumerism." This means, generally, that those who market goods and services are considered under obligation to make sure that the consumer is satisfied in the broadest sense with the transaction. In the early twentieth century this kind of attitude developed as part of the normal and healthy competition in the marketplace between different purveyors. Thus the expression became popular: "The customer is always right." Nowadays, we see increased emphasis on specific warranties, so as to make clear the rights a consumer has. Moreover, many companies employ quality control or quality assurance officers, to be reasonably certain that goods and services do not reach consumers until it is extremely likely that there will be a high satisfaction level among people who are really getting what they feel they have paid for.

Examples of companies that embody that sort of approach might include the fast-food chains that make sure your hamburger or fried chicken will be made in the same way and taste just as good whether you buy lunch in Milwaukee or London. Another example would be some of the car-rental companies that want to make you as happy at the Denver airport as they would in midtown Manhattan. In a sense, it's the old "brand name" notion, in a different style from its nineteenth-century ancestor, applied to the beginning of the twenty-first century on a global scale with high-tech delivery.

Q. 32. Aren't there still lots of problems, though?

Of course! One that still comes up from time to time is the old "bait and switch game." This typically involves the approach of advertising something of apparently high quality at a low price—for instance, a recent-model used car in apparently good condition with low mileage. That's the sort of thing that brings large numbers of potential buyers onto the car lot or into the auto showroom in search of a bargain. But, all too often, when a particular customer would arrive—you guessed it!—that certain car in the newspaper ad would have "just been sold and driven away!" However, since the buyer had come a long way, the salesperson would "just happen to have another car available"—not quite as good a deal, of course, as the one that got away!

Q. 33. Isn't "bait and switch" a good example of a dishonest, immoral business practice?

You bet it is! It has also become a good example of *illegal* practice in many jurisdictions. To guard against this sort of thing happening—where the so-called bargain never really existed except in a misleading newspaper or TV ad—it is now typically required that the advertising include the license plate or serial number of the vehicle being advertised. That way, potential purchasers who lost out on the alleged bargain would have a way of tracking what happened to the vehicle in question, if they were so inclined. That's a legal remedy that is becoming increasingly popular in the statutes of various jurisdictions.

Q. 34. It sounds as if that would be a case where an immoral activity also becomes illegal, but how does that involve a question of ethics in the sense you have used for that term?

That's an important question, for purposes of distinction. The immoral activity—lying to and thereby manipulating customers—becomes viewed as disruptive to society and not in the best interest of the public. It involves areas of criminal activity, namely fraud and—indirectly—a type of theft: if the dishonest merchant is not actually taking people's money out of their pockets, there is the whole idea of taking more money than the goods in question demand, perhaps by victimizing people who are vulnerable to a variety of "sales pressure" techniques, or, at the very least, taking people's time without any good reason to do so, because what they want to buy really is not available and the purveyor already knows that. But when laws to guard against this kind of practice are passed, that frequently takes place when the ethical sense of a profession (auto dealers in this example) is cultivated to a higher level than it may have been before, when people in the business involved decide that a specific practice is unacceptable and therefore, in their way of thinking, unethical.

Q. 35. But how does that notion come to the fore, by consciousness in the profession or by complaints developing among consumers?

In a sense, it doesn't really matter. It's almost like the question, "Which came first, the chicken or the egg?" What frequently occurs is that the more astute members of a profession or industry, who are often those with a higher sense of morality and obligation toward the public, offer a higher standard of goods and services in the first place, and are quick to point out the shortcomings of those who do not. However, so that this doesn't look like mere sniping between competitors, that sort of discrepancy between different companies becomes part of the public consciousness "from the bottom up" in terms of consumer awareness. Then the industry itself—so as to protect the image of the whole group—tends to adopt ethical standards.

Q. 36. How does this translate into laws and standards of practice concerning "truth in packaging" and "truth in advertising"?

Obviously, the impact is significant. Either as a matter of legal requirement, or in terms of the kinds of ethical expectations just mentioned, people really want to know what they're buying: for instance, whether the drink they purchase is fruit *flavored* or real fruit *juice*, or whether the yogurt is *low* fat or fat *free*. These are things that make a difference to people, and if the advertising or packaging turns out to be misleading, then the people selling the product wind up losing the confidence of the public—and maybe losing a lawsuit in the process!

As time goes on, we read and hear of more and more suits in which members of the consuming public claim they were not given all the information they feel they were entitled to in purchasing goods or services. In the technical terms of law, their complaint is that they were not given full and fair disclosure of all the material facts, which are commonly described by law as those facts that would influence the judgment or decision of a reasonable person.

When material facts are not disclosed, and people suffer damages of some kind because they rely on the representations of the person or company selling a good or service, litigation tends to result, especially when large numbers of plaintiffs gather together. What they are alleging, typically, is fraud. Nobody wants to be accused of that particular "f-word," so many professional and industrial groups adopt internal standards which, hopefully, will minimize situations where an accusation of fraud is likely to arise.

Q. 37. Usually, fraud means simply lying. You seem to understand it in somewhat more complicated terms. Can you spell out what you mean?

There are essentially two basic categories of fraud. The first, which really is lying, is sometimes called *positive* fraud, or saying something which is not true. Under this category would be included the making of representations that have no basis in fact, even if the person making the statement does not know them to be false. Without wishing to demean the many real estate agents who deplore such practices, I think of the real estate agents who say "This place is in great shape" when they know the plumbing and wiring are bad—that's obviously a lie—or who say "The schools in this district are wonderful" when they really haven't investigated the schools and are pretending to know about them. In either of these examples, the person making the statement is asking to be respected as a knowledgeable professional, and to have his or her statements relied upon. So, if someone in fact does rely on those representations and suffers damages as a result, they usually have a good case in a suit for fraud.

Negative fraud, on the other hand, means withholding from someone a material fact, as we have previously mentioned. When the fact in question is one that makes a difference in a decision, and people actually make that decision in a way that turns out to work against them, then they suffer damage and a suit is likely to develop. However, by law and by the ethical standards of many professions (again, real estate is an example), the material fact must be disclosed regardless of whether it would have actually influenced a particular judgment. The material fact is something that consumers or members of the public have a right to, whether or not it makes any difference to them personally. So, merely withholding a material fact on the presumption that "in this case it wouldn't matter anyway" is in itself below the professional standard of care in a good many walks of life (again, real estate for example) and a cause of action so far as the law is concerned.

The law will determine, either by argumentation in court according to the circumstances of a pending case, or by precedents from previous cases, or by reference to statute—or a combination of all of these—what is or is not a material fact. Moreover, the law will tend to

distinguish criminal fraud from negligent fraud, and there will characteristically be different remedies and penalties for each of these.

Criminal fraud is not hard to understand: it means the person
perpetrating the fraud *meant* to do so, for whatever reason of expected
personal gain (making a sale, making more money, etc.). In the case of
negligent fraud, the person responsible failed to make full and fair disclosure of the material facts in the situation, out of negligence, and
should have known better, as to either the investigation or the disclosure of the facts in question; again, to use a real estate example, this
could occur if an agent fails to notice indications of likely problems—
called "red flags" in the trade—concerning a property being sold.

**Q. 38. If fraud means somehow failing to communicate information
that should be given, whether by lying or failing to disclose the
truth, then where do we fit in the whole idea of sharing information
that should not be shared?**

Here, we are talking about "privileged" information. This is
information which someone shares with another under the legitimate
presumption of confidence. Obvious examples are "doctor-patient"
and "attorney-client" privilege, as well as the confidentiality that
obtains between members of the clergy and members of their congregations (the "seal of confession" is of particular significance for the
sacrament of reconciliation among Catholics). If that confidence is
violated, the person who shared the information confidentially has
been violated as well. We are, therefore, dealing with another sort of
dishonesty, in the moral sphere, which has implications ethically, in
terms of what is expected as professional conduct in a given walk of
life. Depending on the statutes in the jurisdiction involved, this sort of
action may also have legal consequences. In any case, we are generally
bound to keep secrets that are entrusted to us as human beings, and
there is a "standard of care" imposed upon us if we are doctors,
lawyers, members of the clergy or involved in certain other professions where there are specific expectations concerning "privileged"
information.

Q. 39. Aren't there some exceptions to the "privilege," though, when some other good or principle overrides the obligation of confidentiality—and if so, how do we deal with those cases?

Yes, there are some exceptions, and they make all of our lives harder and more complicated. Those exceptions tend to occur when an absolute legal obligation takes precedence over the presumption of confidentiality, although it is necessary at first to point out how very seldom this takes place. In the case of the "seal of confession," for instance, Catholic priests would go—and have gone—to their deaths rather than violate that "seal," even when asked by civil law to do so. And as a result of that historical experience, most governments respect the confidentiality of the confessional. Likewise, the laws and courts of our society generally respect the privileged information that comes into the minds of physicians, psychiatrists and attorneys. But I can think of an example where there is an interesting variation on the theme of attorney-client privilege. As one of the Illinois Rules of Professional Conduct states:

> A lawyer shall reveal information about a client to the extent it appears necessary to prevent the client from committing an act that would result in death or serious bodily injury (quoted in *Employee Relations Law Journal,* Vol. 19, No. 1, Summer 1993, pg. 92).

The article in which this quote appears goes on to analyze some of the thinking involved:

> All attorneys know or should know that at certain times in their professional career, they will have to forgo economic gain in order to protect the integrity of the legal profession *(ibid.).*

And as an educator, I know of an exception: In many states and jurisdictions, those who deal with minor children are obliged to report to the local authorities (e.g., "child protective services") any signs of apparent child abuse. The law as I know it places this obligation on teachers, counselors, nurses, coaches and others who deal with boys

and girls under the age of majority (usually eighteen). The requirement, as attorneys have explained it to me, applies to the mere *suspicion* of abuse, which need not be proven in order for the report to be
necessary. And, needless to say, the obligation is present when a minor
"confides" to an adult professional some information which leads to
such a suspicion, even when the minor assumes the conversation will
not be repeated.

Sometimes, as in this kind of situation, it seems that all you can
do is work from the right motivations and instincts, based on a well-
developed conscience formed over the years under a variety of good
influences, and do your best. And sometimes you still can't make it
work perfectly.

**Q. 40. When it comes to complicated issues concerning when to
share information or not, what about the highly publicized late-
1980s practice, on Wall Street, of "insider trading"?**

"Insider trading" got into the headlines after some of the disastrous economic effects of the stock market crash of 1987. In a nutshell,
it has to do with sharing or using information which someone comes
by in a manner presumed privileged or confidential, so that the use of
the information results in securities transactions that could not be made
by reasonably knowledgeable members of the public who do not happen to have the "inside" information. It is a good example of both a
type of behavior with substantial negative consequences for society in
general and, at the same time, an activity viewed differently by the ethical and legal perspectives of different countries in the same global
economy. So, if you want a complicated issue, from a moral, ethical
and legal point of view, you can't pick a much better one than "insider
trading."

To see this in perspective, we would do well to look for a
moment at the definition of professional duty for securities brokers
offered in a recent article in the *Journal of Business Ethics:*

> The duty that is relevant for a standard case analysis of
> inside trading...centers upon a relationship of trust and
> confidence that insiders owe to owner/shareholders. The

position or status of the insider, and of someone who has knowingly received a tip from the insider, may place that person in possession of material, non-public information that shareholders and others do not have access to, and could not legally acquire. Abuse of this position of trust keys the elements of fraud that insiders inflict upon shareholders and other investors, and, in order to avoid this breach of trust, insiders must "disclose or abstain from trading" (9:913, 1990).

"Insider trading" stocks were commonly bought and sold through off-shore bank accounts, during the late 1980s, by a variety of "players" in the United States. In one case, for example, the Securities and Exchange Commission (SEC) said a perpetrator had bought 150,000 shares of stock in a company three weeks before the company announced talks of a proposed merger. This enabled the individual, after the merger talks were announced, to make a profit of $2.7 million in selling the stock.

Q. 41. What's wrong with using information you have in order to make intelligent transactions in the stock market?

In general, nothing's wrong with it at all. The problem arises when the information forming the basis of the transaction is learned under an apparent veil of secrecy, or in some privileged context, whereby the information could not be available to people who follow and invest in the market. The net result is that investors don't have a "level playing field."

Q. 42. But what's the problem if nobody really gets hurt?

That is a question asked frequently, in a variety of situations, when folks have trouble visualizing the victims. But in this one instance before us now, of "insider trading," it is apparent at once that there *are* some people who really get hurt. Suppose, for example, that your widowed aunt is living on a fixed income from a pension fund, and the fund invests in the stock market on the advice of a professional investment counselor who follows the market closely. If that fund has to pay more for a stock because its value has been inflated, or is able to sell it for less because its value has been manipulated—as a result of "insider trading"—then the "insiders" have enriched themselves secretly at the expense of your aunt.

The situation is not unlike what took place during the feeding frenzies in real estate during parts of the 1970s and 1980s, when some unscrupulous brokers knew in advance that investors were going to be buying in a given neighborhood, and went around buying up the properties themselves, from families who had owned those homes for years. To make the owners sell, the brokers in question offered them what appeared to be substantial profit but concealed from them the true value that would be realized within a short time. The brokers often pretended to list the properties for sale on the open market, although often they already had made secret plans to purchase the properties for their own accounts. The brokers then made the profit for themselves, and families that had scrimped and saved for years to buy those homes found out too late that they had, in effect, sold short, and would never be able to assist their children in buying homes in an inflated market because they hadn't preserved enough of their equity. It is with this kind of thing in mind that the Code of Ethics of the National Association of Realtors requires its members to disclose a contemplated interest in property which they list or sell (NAR Code of Ethics, Articles 12 and 13). However, some find ways to get around it by making their transactions through friends or relatives with different names as "dummy" buyers and sellers, a practice outlawed in some states as "secret profit" (cf. State of California, Business and Professions Code, # 10176 {g}, {h}; Commissioner's Regulations # 2785 {a}, 11).

Go back now to the example of your widowed aunt. Suppose she had planned to use the equity in her home to help you buy a home near her in the old family neighborhood, but she was hoodwinked by a broker into listing the home for sale at what appeared to be a profit of $100,000 over what she had originally paid for her house—a sum which could help her live in comfort in retirement. However, suppose also that she later learned she could have had almost twice that amount in gain had she known the true value of the home. In such a case, both her retirement income and her chance to help you will suffer. In addition, more and more families like yours are forced out of their neighborhoods and communities are destroyed almost as surely as if freeways were built through them. In the meantime, the broker has long ago taken the money and run off with it, and it's awfully expensive to initiate a lawsuit anyway. Now you see another example of "insider trading" in concrete terms, and it becomes possible to understand why people become so upset with it.

Q. 43. But you indicate that not everyone looks at it the same way, and that there are different expectations and even laws in different places. How does this work?

As a number of experts have pointed out, the "insider" element of insider trading can be changed by consent. In other words, if stockholders themselves agreed to the practice, then the element of damage is not the same as it has been until now, a *fiduciary* relationship (one of trust) has not been breached, and fraud is not present. Moreover, different countries will view the practice in ways that are not necessarily the same as that of the United States. As pointed out in the same analysis quoted earlier, from the *Journal of Business Ethics:*

> As a matter of fact, many of our trading partners view inside trading with more tolerance, perhaps annoyance, than alarm...Germany, for example, relies on voluntary guidelines enforced (or not) by business firms through employment contracts. Inside trades are not illegal. France and Japan have limited prohibitions, but, as different as those cultures are, there is a certain leniency in their treatment of inside trading. In France this practice is part of the business culture and is hardly considered immoral. Japan prohibits it, but with evident lack of enthusiasm *(ibid.).*

In other words, different societies have different standards and different "rules of the road" for this sort of practice. Each of the nations involved has the right to make its own laws about such things.

Q. 44. This seems like a potentially costly way of doing business, though, especially at a time when many companies want to remain competitive in the worldwide economy. How does a company survive and hold onto its market share in competition with companies from other nations when the ethical standards and laws differ?

Obviously, this is a problem that will do nothing but become more complex before it becomes simplified. Only recently, we have seen politics begin to catch up with technology in the increasing development of what has so often been called the "global village." As people have become used to communicating around the world with cellular phones and fax machines, and holding interactive intercontinental face-to-face meetings with videotelephones, it is only natural that we will see different nations join together into common markets of one sort or another. The North American Free Trade Agreement [NAFTA] is one example of this; the "United States of Europe" or "EC" has been another, making the old European Common Market of the late 1950s seem primitive by comparison. And, of course, the countries of North and South America are going to have more and more roles and responsibilities in participating in an economy that is based on both sides of the Pacific Rim. As such developments continue, it will be necessary for there to be more and more discussion about business ethics, to fine tune the expectations that can be held in common by different countries, so that there can be fair and manageable agreement on what the rules are for doing business.

Q. 45. But you have been explaining many things in terms of the ethical standards of American business. Given the differences between various cultures and countries, can people in the United States afford to compete in a global economy?

They can't afford not to. What has made imported goods so popular in the United States, for example, has been the fact that they are made well and sold at attractive prices. This gives American manufacturers and sales forces a "tough act to follow." Competition in itself is usually considered an incentive to quality in goods and services; it's part of what makes a capitalistic economy productive and successful.

Q. 46. Is it possible that nations like the United States can continue successfully as capitalistic market economies without causing or perpetuating an unequally stratified society with the "lower classes" essentially stuck where they are?

To say that this sort of consideration poses serious dilemmas is to make a gross understatement. It is patently obvious that profit in some highly developed economies, like that of the United States and some other nations, relies on very inexpensive labor from other countries. The "cheapness" of that labor comes from more than the mere difference in monetary values between nations. As a matter of fact, those monetary values reflect the more important difference, which is in purchasing power. The "bottom line" is that a lower standard of living, or quality of life, is able to be purchased by many workers in "third world" labor markets than by workers in the United States and other industrialized nations who buy the products made by their "third world" neighbors.

Also, the labor of some of these countries often involves children, who about a century ago began to be protected by the law, in nations like the United States and the United Kingdom, against having to work under "sweatshop" conditions when they should be in school and otherwise properly cared for as juveniles.

Q. 47. Does this mean that the average person in a country like the United States, for instance, should stop buying products which are made with "cheap" labor, until working and living conditions in the other countries involved have improved?

It's hardly that simple. The difficult fact is that many of the people buying such products—sports shirts, athletic shoes, slacks, just to name some examples in the line of clothing—are doing so to save money as they themselves live under economic limitations—layoffs, "downsizing," inflation in the costs of housing and education—while they are trying to provide for their children as are their fellow human beings in those other countries we speak of. As a matter of fact, many Americans and others are now wearing such relatively inexpensive garments, when they used to purchase more elaborate and expensive ones.

Moreover, such consumers as I have just described often have great difficulty finding comparable products made by unionized or otherwise well-compensated workers, at any price, because so many of the manufacturing jobs, at least on the assembly line, have left countries like the United States to go to other markets in terms of cheaper labor. And that fact in itself makes it harder for the average working person in the United States to support himself/herself and a family.

Perhaps a better answer lies in asking that companies produce goods at a realistic cost that includes the value of labor in a fair context. This will mean a better "package" of compensation and benefits for the assembly-line or factory-type worker, wherever he or she works. Of necessity, there will have to be a moderate increase in the price of the goods on the market. But that will not be enough to make up the difference. The ultimate solution has to involve a reduction in the compensation and benefits given to the very few people at the top of the pyramid in many manufacturing or other companies, and there is obvious resistance to this on the part of some very powerful executives in American companies, where the gap between the chief executive officers and the lowest-paid workers seems far greater than in other major industrialized nations of the world, such as Japan.

Q. 48. But in terms of competition between—say—Japan and the United States, aren't there real differences in the relationship between the employer and the employee that have an effect on how all this works out?

Definitely. And here is how we begin to see some ethical questions regarding the rights and obligations of employer and employee to each other.

Part V

ETHICS IN THE WORKPLACE—
OBLIGATIONS FOR EMPLOYERS
AND EMPLOYEES

Q. 49. Specifically, what does an employer owe to a worker?

In the purest sense, "a fair day's wage for a fair day's work." But the relationship becomes more complicated when the work and the wage are for more than a day. Then other questions arise. The first question to be considered, in my opinion, is whether the employment is understood by both parties to be long-term or temporary.

In the case where both the employer and employee understand the relationship to be of an emergency, short-term or temporary nature, then we can usually presume that the employee gives up relatively little in terms of other opportunities to make a living. As a consequence, there should be little or no obligation on the part of the employer for the future of the employee, beyond abiding by reasonable conditions for the health and safety of the worker on the job, and other understandable elements of fair dealing. In other words, short term employment is usually based on an agreed-upon wage, with few, if any, additional benefits (insurance, pension, etc.).

On the other hand, the employee seeking a permanent job, who commits himself or herself to an employer for a long period of time—perhaps including some time spent in preparation or training—pays something for the opportunity of this particular job, in terms of letting other opportunities go by. This is what courts have tended to find in cases of "wrongful discharge." The principle involved includes an implied "good faith" covenant of continued employment so long as the employee performs satisfactorily and the employer is not in such financial peril that the employee is really unaffordable.

Q. 50. How do expectations concerning compensation and benefits tend to vary with the anticipated length of the employment relationship?

If an employment situation is by its nature an "emergency" or "fill-in" hire, the employee does not usually expect such benefits as

61

pension plans. On the other hand, if the work is of such intensity or danger that the employee gives up some other opportunity or takes on significant risk in order to accept the job, then there is some compensation that the employee expects to receive and the employer should expect to provide, even if the assignment is of short duration. That seems to be the reasoning behind some of the higher salaries and benefits packages involved in occupations which by their nature are physically dangerous—such as working with certain hazardous materials—or which tend to "burn out" employees after a relatively short time. In some other jobs it seems that the benefits earned by long-term employees tend to accrue more gradually. On the other hand, there are some jobs in which such benefits as insurance, pension vesting and the like become available immediately, because the employee agrees to work full-time, and therefore forsake the opportunity to earn the money to pay for these benefits in some other way. This means the employer finds it less expensive to provide the benefits for the employee as part of a group than to simply pay a much higher salary and allow the employee to contract for such things outside the workplace.

Perhaps a simpler way of addressing this kind of question is to say that the more an employee puts into an employment relationship, the more he or she expects to get out of it, not only in terms of salary, but in a variety of other benefits (job security, health insurance and the like) as well.

Q. 51. It seems there could be some loopholes there. Don't some employers keep turning over equally qualified personnel in the same job category, consecutively, so as to avoid making permanent commitments?

Yes, unfortunately. If this kind of thing demonstrates a pattern, it is arguably an evasion of moral obligation to employees. That would be true in terms of the moral values of most religious belief systems (including Christianity) and many individuals, even though it may not present a problem in terms of the prevailing ethic of many employers—driven by the cost-cutting functions of the overriding profit motive—in today's marketplace. Depending on the circumstances of the case, it may also be a way around legal responsibility. When a series of "revolving door" part-time or short-term employees, who would be qualified for permanent full-time work with full benefits, parade into and out of a workplace as a convenience to an employer who need never worry about the costs involved in permanent workers, then something is unfair, and ultimately there are considerable social costs. The same is true when several long-term part-time workers are hired to fill what amounts to one or two full-time workers' positions, again so as to avoid various benefits and commitments. Then, as Shakespeare wrote, "Something is rotten in the State of Denmark!" As reported by the Bulletin of the American Association of Retired Persons (AARP) in 1992, this kind of employment situation especially affects senior citizens who are not yet eligible for retirement benefits and are on the job market in competition with others who are younger and less expensive:

> ...most people holding "contingent" jobs get low pay, receive few benefits and, perhaps most troubling of all, enjoy little or no job security. All too often, such jobs end abruptly, with little or no warning. Yet, contingent work is on the rise. Consisting of part-time, temporary, contract and various types of free-lance jobs, the contingent labor force grew faster than full-time employment during the 1980s....Normally full-timers, they work at contingent jobs because they're the only kind they can get (*AARP Bulletin*, Vol. 33, No. 5, May, 1992, pg. 2).

In fact, this sort of issue has become an area of recent concern on the part of some U.S. Congress members. As a result, this may take on the dimensions of a legal issue as well as a moral one.

It is possible, then, that both the civil authorities as well as the employees are being defrauded. At least some civil authorities seem to think that is possibly the case. As cited by the AARP, some legislators are worried about

> ...a "serious, widespread and growing" problem: the misclassification of workers as independent contractors when they are actually regular employees....Companies use this device to escape paying Social Security and unemployment

compensation taxes, and to avoid the costs of withholding federal and state income taxes. The disadvantage for employees: They have to pay the employer's share (7.65 percent) of Social Security taxes, and they lose some protections of federal labor laws (*ibid.*).

But stingy employers are also very clever, and often tend to categorize people as "part-time" when they work only so many hours a week, then make sure to offer fewer hours per week to each of a number of employees, actually reducing their opportunity to earn a living, just in order to avoid the legal obligations of benefits and security. This is often true, especially, in many colleges and universities where shrewd administrators have taken advantage of their supply-and-demand position in light of the "teacher glut" when it has come to hiring new faculty over the last twenty or so years. This trend was addressed recently at an institute for part-time faculty sponsored by the California Federation of Teachers, AFT/AFL-CIO, and reported in their newsletter:

> • In the '50s and '60s, part-timers comprised about 12–15% of faculty and were mostly "specialists" in vocational fields.

> • Funding cutbacks in the '70s, coupled with explosive enrollment growth, led colleges to increase reliance on cheap part-time labor.

> …1979: Supreme Court ruled on the Peralta Suit, establishing the 60% standard as the demarcation between part-time and full-time faculty.

> …Today…the percentage of part-time faculty rises to more than 60, with 35–50% of all Community College classes continuing to be taught by underpaid, overworked, unsupported part-timers (*Perspective*, Vol. 25, No. 3, February, 1994, pgs. 1, 4, 5).

Q. 52. So, are you arguing that, from a moral perspective, except for demonstrably temporary situations, some permanent job security with full benefits is a basic right—is that correct?

Some folks' moral vision wants me to give you a simple "yes" to that, but in light of some of the accepted ethical norms and civil laws in our society it's not always *quite* that simple. Once more, one needs to look at whether the conduct of the employer and employee would logically lead to the reasonable presumption of a long-term relationship and the forsaking of other opportunities. Moreover, as more and more employers in a competitive economic atmosphere feel they are unable, or are unwilling, to offer permanent employment—because of mergers, takeovers or adverse economic conditions—more and more employees are seeking employment elsewhere, when they might not have considered this in the economy of the past.

This means that the relationships between employers and employees are changing substantially, at least in the United States and in some other countries as well. To elaborate: the implied covenant of job security usually went hand in hand with another implied covenant of employee loyalty, both of which have been evolving in recent years.

It is commonly said that in Japan, an employment relationship is by its nature usually a long-term one, with mutual loyalties. In the United States, something like that two-sided faithfulness once tended to be the case as well, so that an employee going to work for an employer's competitor—or just not staying until retirement—was frequently viewed as a type of betrayal. This kind of model also has prevailed for a long time in most of the industrialized countries of Europe. But the model just described now seems to be more and more a relic of the past, even across the Pacific and Atlantic oceans from the United States.

These days in America, it is more commonly the case that employees are not expected to stay with one employer for an entire working lifetime, just as an employer is not necessarily expected to keep an employee from hire date through retirement. The subject of loyalty in the workplace was discussed in a most interesting way by Jesuit ethicist John C. Haughey, shortly after the beginning of the 1990s:

> Loyalties are affections. As affections they are initially
> premoral. Once they are chosen and acted upon, of course,

they become moral and significant fonts of behavior....We
need to be loyal, it seems, because we need to live for
more than ourselves and pursue an agenda beyond ourselves....Loyalty to a company, therefore, is a response to
being heard, to being valued, to being cared about.
Unilateral loyalty doesn't last long or doesn't happen
[Emphasis added] (*America,* Vol. 164, No. 17, May 4,
1991, pg. 490).

**Q. 53. Does all this mean that in today's society the employer and
employee really should not expect to have any permanent
obligations to each other?**

No. It isn't that simple. From the sheer standpoint of "good business," I believe, it means that whatever *can* be done to encourage
worker loyalty—providing the employer expects the employee to
remain on the job awhile—*should* be done, because that winds up
being to the benefit of the employer as well as the employee. Also, it
benefits indirectly the members of the public who have come to rely
on the goods or services provided by the employer. As Haughey con-
tinues:

Who has not known the undesirable condition of a work
situation that is bereft of loyalty?...If some degree of loyalty does not undergird the worker/boss relationship, it
would be naive to think that a work force would be motivated to do a full day's work for a day's pay simply out of
a sense of responsibility. Where there is little or no identi-
fication with the place where one works or the people for
whom one works, corners are easily cut, leaving management with little alternative than to hire more workers (thus
upping the cost of products to consumers) or to fire their
employees more easily (rapid turnover is not going to generate more loyalty). *The fact that a company eliciting little
or no loyalty from its workers fails to make the ethically
egregious list in the media does not mean that the place is
ethically sound* [Emphasis added].

...Before one gets cynical about workplace loyalties, it is good to remember the good that usually accrues from them....To work for more than simply keeping one's job, to work for more than getting a salary, to work with one's affectivity caught up in doing as good a job as possible, is a highly desirable state of affairs for both employee and employer....Conversely, the absence of solidarity in the workplace is costly (*ibid.*, pg. 491).

Q. 54. It sounds as though you—or Haughey—could be making subtle threats here, against employers on behalf of employees, in terms of "sick-outs," sabotage and the like. Is that any kind of "ethical" or moral position to take?

I fear you misunderstand the context of either Haughey's words, or mine, or both. I don't advocate the kinds of negative behavior just mentioned, nor do I believe he does. I do believe, though, that what is being described here is the predictable tendency of human nature to respond to the feeling of being insecure or devalued. This sort of thing seems to be happening in a variety of workplaces, when people feel that their wholehearted involvement will not generate the sort of security and other benefits they had hoped for when they entered the job market. They necessarily spend a good deal of time and energy looking for the next job that will have to take the place of the present one when the present one is no longer available or viable for them. This is, as Haughey and others suggest, costly for the employer, even short of the obvious abuses committed by some employees, like petty theft and malingering.

Q. 55. So are you saying you can see examples of immoral behavior on the part of some employees?

Regrettably, there are many such examples. I don't even mean things like embezzlement, which are so major and obvious that they don't need to be mentioned here. I am thinking of little things like using the office photocopier or telephone for personal business, taking home stationery supplies, and other things which are in fact a form of theft from the employer (unless, of course, the employer's permission is given for such a thing). Somewhat bigger offenses include cheating on time sheets, and taking excessively long breaks or lunch hours (meaning beyond the time allowed for them). This doesn't mean an employer cannot or never should allow for some flexibility, particularly in cases of emergency or to compensate for unpaid overtime or unusual effort. But when employees take objects, services or time which is not theirs, then they are stealing.

Q. 56. Does this mean, then, that the presumption of permanent employment, complete with full benefits, should be a reasonable expectation of every employee in order to avoid negative behavior and ensure cooperation?

No. It means that one needs to look at the agreements that are made between the parties, not only in express contracts but also the ones that are implied by the conduct of the employer and the employee, to learn what they could reasonably have expected of each other. At least, those seem to be the criteria most frequently relied upon in "wrongful discharge" or "unlawful termination" complaints.

One factor that would be involved, as mentioned before, would be the length and intensity of the employee's preparation for the job. This is significant because preparing for a career or profession is expensive not only in direct monetary costs (tuition in school, etc.) but also in indirect costs (opportunity for salary which is not earned while preparing oneself). To use an example from the teaching profession: since teachers at various levels spend considerable time, energy and money acquiring the qualifications for their positions, it has traditionally been considered fair for the schools that employ them to offer permanent situations (i.e., "tenure") to those who have completed a period of probation (typically several years).

However, in today's world when someone suitable as a teacher for five or ten years is not necessarily suitable for *forty* years, various schools and school systems are modifying the traditional "tenure" program (over half a century old) and hiring approved teachers for stated periods of time. Such periods, usually renewable, are often in increments of up to five or more years. In any case, the employee has some idea of where he or she stands and what can be expected, rather than be subject to capricious dismissal or replacement. Professional associations and unions in a variety of occupations have sought, and often achieved, similar protection for their members. Their premise is that it is only fair for employers to let their employees know what is likely to lie ahead in consideration of the commitment they have made.

Put simply and bluntly: no teacher, nurse, or other professional would want to spend a number of years away from the full-time job market, paying tuition and taking classes to qualify for a job that can be terminated in a year or two simply because the employer can hire another person who is less experienced and therefore less expensive. Moreover, this sort of "turnover," while perhaps economical for the employer in the short term, does not serve the employer's clientele (students, patients, etc.) in the long run.

The same argument can be advanced for various kinds of skilled laborers, craftsmen, and so forth.

Q. 57. The case for reasonable job security having been made, what do employers owe to employees in terms of a "living wage," assuming the employees will use prudently the wages paid to them, making reasonable provision for themselves and their obligations to any dependents they may have?

Most people would agree, in fairness, that basic human dignity in most job situations means being able to live as well as other people live who perform a similar kind of work in the same community, provided that certain minimal needs are met. Most would agree also that these needs include the ability to procure: the kind of shelter which—whether owned or rented—meets basic requirements of health and safety; the sort of food that provides for a balanced diet which is adequate to ensure reasonably good health; the kind of clothing which is in keeping with what others wear in the same society; the level of health care that can reasonably be expected as available to the people in the area for not only curing but preventing illness.

Q. 58. If all those things are done, does the employee then have an obligation to remain available to the same employer under similar conditions?

That is a perfectly logical question. We cannot answer it simply by saying that the employee has a lifelong obligation to the employer, or even one that cannot ever be broken during a long contractual period. Otherwise we would be talking about slavery or indentured servitude, and violating the employee's right to "shop" or try to "sell" his or her qualifications elsewhere in the open market.

However, as most employers try to spell out in contracts, there are certain standards of loyalty owed them by persons on their payroll, at least while the relationship is in effect. For example, an employer will often prohibit a full-time employee from holding another job. This is often reasonable, due to the negative effect "moonlighting" could have on the availability, energy and diligence of the employee. In some cases employers will forbid employees to engage in certain activities deemed injurious to their effectiveness or the image of the employer. An example would be some professional sports teams, which prohibit players from smoking in uniform when they can be seen by fans (even though some players smoke privately). Another instance would be railroads and airlines which require their crews to be free from the influence of alcohol or other drugs when performing their duties. Obviously, an employer has a right to insist that an employee not work for a direct competitor during the time of the employment relationship.

Q. 59. If the employee does leave, can he or she fairly go to work for a competitor, or can the employer enforce certain "covenants not to compete" that run for some years after an employee leaves?

The type of "covenant not to compete" you mention is sometimes part of an employment contract. Its most frequent use, in my experience, occurs when a business is sold and the previous owner agrees to not open his own competing business within a certain period of time and within a certain geographical radius (thus it is often called a "radius clause" in a contract). This is paid for as part of the "goodwill" element in the value of the business opportunity being sold. And closely allied to it, very often, is the former business owner's agree-

ment to work as an employee of the new owner, under a "personal services" contract, in order to help get the business on the right track
under the new ownership.

Sometimes, though, an employer will force an employee, as a
condition of hiring or of continued employment, to sign a "non-compe-
tition" agreement, stating that he or she will not work for a competing
company for a given period of time after the present employment relationship ends. This is a subject of some legal controversy in case law,
precisely because of the issues surrounding the rights of the individual
and "restraint of trade." Clearly, someone who reports on areas of his
or her expertise for a newspaper would be in a "conflict of interest" by
writing for a competing publication at the same time. But such people
would have a right to leave the one when their contract expires, and go
to work for the other if they so wish.

One way employers can prevent employees from working for
competitors, of course, is to make the terms of employment so attractive and hard to duplicate that employees are not motivated to leave.
Another way is to pay out the term of an extended contract, even when
the employee's services are no longer strictly required, to keep that
employee from working for a competitor. To use another example
from the media industry, one TV network reportedly did this with a
popular comedian in the years after World War II, to keep him from
appearing on a competing network.

**Q. 60. The issue of "trade secrets" is often mentioned; what does
that mean and how does it figure in here?**

It's sometimes very important, in the context of what is called
"intellectual property" as a legal concept. To use the newspaper
reporter's story again: If former employees of one paper leave to go to
work for another, can they divulge to their new employer those things
which they have learned about a competitor in a confidential relationship? Or can they use under a new employer some idea, material or
information which they developed under the old one—such as leads
for business? The question needs to be evaluated morally, legally and
ethically.

Morally, we are generally under obligation to keep confidential those pieces of information communicated to us with the expectation they will be maintained as secrets.

Legally, the enforceability of "trade secret" covenants in employment contracts seems to have come down to this: Employers probably can prohibit former employees from using information they have learned as employees, providing the material really is *secret* and would not have been learned in some other context anyway. However, there are typically time limitations on such agreements: secrets begin to lose their economic value as they become older, and the information either becomes obsolete or begins to acquire the status of common knowledge rather than privileged information.

Ethically (i.e., relying on commonly acceptable behavior within a profession or occupation), it is important to be aware of what the standards of behavior are among a group of people who share concern for the well-being of their trade and their public. Codes of ethics for journalists, teachers, accountants, etc., usually provide "rules of the road" to be applied to particular situations.

Q. 61. With all the factors that have been mentioned, it is apparent that the workplace of today can be a very stressful environment for people as individuals, and especially as members of families. In addition, the stress can really test the faith of people who want to hold onto religious and moral beliefs and principles. What can be done in the workplace to be of help to such people?

Many employers today are coming to recognize that employee illnesses—whether physical, psychological or emotional—cost a great deal in terms of productivity, not only in the short term but also over the long run. With that realization in mind, many employers offer employee assistance programs [EAP's] or "wellness" programs. Put crudely, many employers realize that it makes sense to keep employees in efficient running order like machines. On a higher plane, it can be said that the overall cultivation of a humane workplace ultimately increases productivity and generates goodwill among employees and customers alike. In the same vein, a good many employers have made their workers' lives less frantic by providing various forms of day care for employees' children, and similar parent-friendly programs like "flex-time" that will allow for child-care schedules apart from the workplace. In addition many employers now offer "parent education" or "parenting" classes during lunch hours or at other convenient times, sometimes in cooperation with a local community college or other agency. While it might be said that none of these things is a strict obligation in justice, all of them seem to show respect for the needs of the employees as human beings and for the value of an individual person and his or her family, in keeping with the principles of virtually every religious and moral tradition known to humanity. In point of fact, though, it can also be observed that some collective bargaining agreements [CBA's] now refer to such programs as we have just considered, regarding them as benefits to be bargained for in negotiations between employers and unions. That should give an idea of how important such things are!

As to the strength of a worker's religious faith or spiritual life, it is here that the role of an employer should be almost certainly one of permissiveness and nothing more, allowing for bereavement leave in keeping with one's religious tradition when a loved one dies (requiring more time, characteristically, for Buddhists or Jews than for adherents of other religions), or for time off (perhaps with leave or on a "comp time" arrangement) for important family religious observances or holy days (Jewish, Christian, etc.). Beyond that, it seems the responsibility of organized religion to make its services available to people in a variety of workplaces. Among Catholics, this has long been done by a variety of "downtown churches" that offer early-morning or lunch-hour masses (by orders like the Franciscans, Paulists or Jesuits, especially, in cities like New York, San Francisco, Milwaukee, etc.); many Protestant clergy and laity have organized groups like the Wall Street Prayer Breakfast in New York, and so on, often with a major corporation providing a meeting place. It's all part of humanizing the workplace and meeting people where they are.

Q. 62. While some of the above considerations seem to make good sense, aren't there possibilities for employers to intrude excessively into the private lives of their workers?

Of course. This is why, when some conditions of employment are considered to be excessive, they are put to a common-sense legal test as to whether or not these things are a necessary element of job performance. The classic example would be "morals clauses," which for decades were in effect (explicitly or implicitly) as conditions for various kinds of employment. A case in point: It is essential to virtually any job to require that employees not be under the influence of alcohol or other drugs while on duty. However, it is hard to justify the legality of insisting that they have never used such substances in their lives, or will never do so when off duty (providing there is no residual effect on job performance). Many employers and managers whose views on such issues are more conservative may be upset to learn that they cannot control employees' behavior to the extent they would wish to, but there are some individual freedoms which employers cannot abridge.

Likewise, many employers and managers may disapprove of certain living arrangements entered into by some of their employees, e.g., unmarried, with live-in lovers of the opposite sex or same sex. But such disapproval does not give the employer the right to regulate this aspect of workers' lives or violate their right to individual conscience. This is true not only from a legal point of view, but in the moral context of many religions' teachings on religious liberty, including the Roman Catholic Church's declaration on this issue from the Second Vatican Council.

Q. 63. But don't some of those same religious organizations, including the Roman Catholic Church, have the right when they employ people to insist on certain standards of care for such personnel—clergy, teachers, and so forth—as role models?

I would argue strongly that they do, if they believe that certain behaviors are inconsistent with the responsibilities of the position in question. Nobody, I hope, wants an athletic coach in the Catholic Youth Organization who believes that the best way to win a game is by cheating. Besides that obvious example, most folks feel that anyone who leads youth, even in such seemingly technical areas as the teaching of algebra, should not model behavior which contradicts the teaching of a value-oriented institution such as a religious school. People tend to agree that private, religious organizations have the right to expect certain standards of visible behavior from their employees, which is why very few such institutions, if any, would want to be known as harboring a sexist or racist on their payrolls. Such a person, in today's atmosphere, would be hard pressed to win an employment situation of a "high profile" nature in almost any place.

However, many religious institutions which have a variety of functions that are not specifically religious, such as schools, try to attract both students and staff who are not necessarily devout, practicing members of that particular religious denomination. When that is the case, it is very hard to enforce any sort of "morals clause" beyond that which would be expected of any member of the larger society. So, while it is certainly the right and duty of a religious school—or any school—to dismiss a teacher or coach who is a child abuser, it is not so clear that they could get rid of one who is a cigarette smoker, even if that particular religion forbids the practice, unless the teacher violates a local health ordinance by smoking in a prohibited area (classroom, playground, etc.).

Like it or not, gone are the days (if they truly existed completely) when all the students at a Lutheran school are Lutheran, all at a Roman Catholic school are Roman Catholic, and so on. There are Jews attending Quaker schools, Buddhists attending Baptist schools, and people with no formal religion attending Episcopalian schools. And the schools themselves seek individual, corporate and foundation support from donors who are not adherents of their particular religions and who abhor some of the restrictions of "morals clauses." When that is the case, it becomes very hard to enforce such limits on the behavior of employees, especially when they are "on their own time." Some of the people attending or supporting the school who are devout members of the religion in question may be very upset about this, but it appears their point of view does not prevail in most "religious" schools today, which in fact are more likely private institutions with religious heritages and constituencies, as distinct from the sorts of "yeshivas" and "seminaries" many of us knew from yesteryear.

Q. 64. Speaking of the specific viewpoint of a religious context, what, then, are the *moral* obligations of an employer owed to an employee?

If you ask humanists who deal in the social sciences, like Abraham Maslow, they would speak of the basic human needs of shelter, clothing and food as essential to human dignity. If you consult the social teachings of the Roman Catholic Church over the last century and more, you would find essentially the same considerations. The popes who wrote the "social encyclicals," from Leo XIII in 1891 through John Paul II a century later, have spoken of a decent place to live, food and clothing, as requisites for treating someone with dignity. In particular, Pope John XXIII reflected the thinking of many religious traditions besides his own when he wrote in *Mater et Magistra* [1961]:

> ...workers must be paid a wage which allows them to live a truly human life and to fulfill their family obligations in a worthy manner. Other factors too enter into the assessment of a just wage: namely, the effective contribution which each individual makes to the economic effort, the financial state of the company for which he works, the requirements of the general good of the particular country—having regard especially to the repercussions on the overall employment of the working force in the country as a whole—and finally the requirements of the common good of the universal family of nations of every kind, both large and small [n. 71].

Q. 65. So, are employers in fact obliged to do what Maslow and the religious leaders suggest?

From the standpoint of Christian morality, I would say so. From the standpoint of the Jewish tradition, which has for so many centuries put a premium on justice in the social order, I would again answer in the affirmative. From the viewpoint of Hinduism, one of whose chief exponents was Mohandas K. Gandhi, I would once more answer with a resounding "Yes." And I would say the same against the background of many another religious tradition. In sum, you could say that the sort of ethic that has been inculcated in me—from a variety of theological sources—all adds up to answer that question positively.

But then we come to the question of whether or not employers will see their obligations clearly. This is a classic case of how personal morality so frequently collides with the ethic of a business community concerned with the "bottom line." As with so many other things, there really are no simple answers. This is because there are some variations on the theme from time to time and from place to place.

Q. 66. How can the conditions for living with dignity, and the obligations of employers, vary? Can you illustrate this?

Let's take, for example, the areas of clothing and shelter. For instance, concerning clothing: many employers in Great Britain provide a wardrobe allowance for their personnel, who are expected to be dressed according to certain standards there. Such a benefit is even considered non-taxable income by the British government, since it is so commonly expected that it is expensive for employees in certain classifications to be outfitted according to the dress codes of their employers. In most other places, such an expectation does not apply. If workers are allowed to come to the job site wearing casual, inexpensive clothes they could wear for other purposes, then it is probably not reasonable to expect that they be given a specific clothing allowance.

In some places it is common for workers to own their own homes, and thus an employee who works for a given firm over a certain period of time might reasonably expect to accumulate a down payment on a home in the area, as a result of prudent saving, and to enjoy the sort of regular income that would allow for financing a home purchase. In many other areas, home ownership is rare, and perhaps a more reasonable expectation is a salary which allows for renting a suitable place to live that is not too far from the work site.

Q. 67. Isn't it possible, though, that employers could utilize the economic principle of supply-and-demand to force employees to accept ever-diminishing standards of living?

This is always a factor in the marketplace, and as time goes on the balance could shift in favor of employers. In that kind of situation there is a danger that power and not principle will be the governing factor. In the same document we referred to before, Pope John XXIII remarked:

...the remuneration of work is not something that can be left to the laws of the marketplace; nor should it be a decision left to the will of the more powerful. It must be determined in accordance with justice and equity...[*loc. cit.*].

In practicality, though, the economic world does not march to the tune of any religious leader, regardless of how large the denomination which appears to be represented. And, in the relationship between employers and employees, many observers suggest that the balance of the supply-and-demand equation has already begun working in favor of employers, in a way which was not true as recently as a generation ago.

As time goes on, it becomes increasingly likely that employers will bring workers from elsewhere to undercut the wage levels of local employees. As a consequence, a community which is relatively stable, including many families who own homes, could become a community of people who move in and out for jobs and who rent apartments or houses for the short term. People who feel a sense of roots and ownership in a community tend to become displaced and dispersed.

Q. 68. Are there consequences to society, when this happens, over and above those directly affecting the employer-employee relationship?

I certainly think so. For instance, in his book of many years ago entitled *A Nation of Strangers,* American social critic Vance Packard wrote that people who transfer into and out of communities for employment opportunities are often good workers but poor citizens. By this he didn't mean that they are lawbreakers, but that they tend not to make long-term investments in communities where they don't expect to remain. As a result, these are folks who often don't register to vote, since they develop no familiarity or concern with local candidates and issues. Or, when they do vote, they have a short-term interest in keeping their taxes down. As a result, they vote against issues which have long-term benefits for the community, like school and hospital improvements.

Q. 69. Does this suggest, then, that employers have obligations to contribute to the stability of the areas in which they do business?

It does, with the idea that the people who live in that area—whether or not they are employees or customers of the employer—have some vested interest in the social impact of that employer's business. However, we are dealing here in the area of moral values which are essentially a matter of personal priorities, and perhaps in the area of ethical sensibilities concerning an employer's role in a community. We are not talking about any fixed law here.

Part VI

STOCKHOLDERS AND STAKEHOLDERS—
ETHICAL OBLIGATIONS BETWEEN
COMPANIES AND COMMUNITIES

Q. 70. Even so, then doesn't it follow that employers in general would be well advised to consider the communities where they do business as partners in their enterprises?

I would certainly say so. Although a company typically has "stockholders," it also has "stakeholders" in the community which provide a positive atmosphere—a workforce, an environment, a market—for the company. This means the company has some obligation to these "stakeholders," morally, as well as to its "stockholders," financially, in making business decisions. This moral obligation frequently takes the form of civil laws having to do with safety codes, the cleanup of toxic waste, and other environmental concerns. But it is in a sense more basic.

Put simply, the company needs not just to take something from the local community, but to put something back in, over and above just obeying the laws and paying taxes.

Q. 71. Other than performing voluntary acts of charity, like contributing to a community fund for the poor or sponsoring a blood drive, what sorts of things should a company do for the community where it does business?

Here it is evident the word "should" presupposes certain moral values, like the ones embodied in the bible and which various religious bodies have espoused in different ways. But if one holds such values, and others of like mind make their feelings known, they would ask certain things of the employers in their community.

One thing, clearly, is to employ qualified people in the community who are seeking work, rather than to "colonize" the community by bringing in an excessive number of "outside hires."

Q. 72. If people are already employed by a company that moves or establishes a new location, don't they have a right to bring their

experience and dedication with them to that site? And doesn't their employer have the right to take advantage of their proven worth?

It would seem so, but sometimes the company, rather than move existing employees to a new workplace, simply casts its net around the country or around the world, passing over qualified residents of the local community in search of cheaper labor. When this happens, the local community's unemployment rates and costs of housing and governmental services tend to go up at the same time. It's a terrible combination. And this tends to happen in a great many cities and towns all over, as more and more companies look for inexpensive land, low taxes, minimal government regulation and cheap labor.

Q. 73. In other words, social responsibility to the local community could be considered as a cost of doing business?

Yes. It may not be a directly calculated cost like municipal business taxes, but it can be a legitimate cost of operation just the same.

The idea here is not unrelated, I think, to some religious notions of the obligations of wealth. Jews and Christians have long advocated setting aside a percentage of one's income—often ten percent or a "tithe" for the Lord, or for the work of the Lord in behalf of the less fortunate in society; Muslims express a similar notion as one of the five pillars of Islam. But whether one is religiously-motivated or not, such a thing makes good sense for a business that plans to operate in a community.

Q. 74. Whether or not civil laws mandate such considerations, should the business community think about cultivating an ethic based on moral values supported by the place where they earn money?

I think the argument for that can surely be made, first on the grounds mentioned before that the community has a stake in the business. But this should not be looked at as a one-way street. Remember that if the company doesn't benefit the place where they operate, they won't have an economic base. People who live near the company's sites—especially those who have been on the short end economically—will be resentful, and this will find a way to show itself in the marketplace.

Q. 75. Many countries around the world rely heavily on child labor, without the kinds of restrictions and protections found in nations like the United States. Is it morally acceptable for the United States or other countries to be partners in trade with them?

Many people would answer that question with an immediate negative, since the concept of child labor is morally repugnant to most of us. We must take into account, practically speaking, the fact that many children and their families would not survive if the children were not employed, even though this is a situation which should be corrected by the payment of a living wage to the parents in such a way that keeps the family together. However, pressure must be brought to bear by those whose vision rejects the exploitation of children and their families.

Q. 76. But with all the many moral value systems out there, and the apparent lack of a common consensus on a lot of these ethical issues involving business, how can one find any kind of measuring stick?

This is a difficult question for each person to answer in his or her own circumstances, to be sure. But there is a famous doctrine of the Buddha which keeps coming to mind, the "principle of right livelihood" which teaches that everyone has a right to make an honest living, but not in a manner so aggressive that it deprives others of their own basic rights. In this context the applications might be like these: the struggling owner of a small business may have to lay off employees when times are hard, but the well-compensated chief executive officer of a major corporation has no business pulling down a six-figure salary when loyal employees are being laid off so as to support the profit margin that makes his paycheck affordable. As noted previously, there's a tremendous gap in the United States—apparently more so than in any other industrialized nation in the world—between what the C.E.O.'s and the rank-and-file employees typically earn, and that is an example of genuine social injustice, in addition to being, ultimately, bad business.

Q. 77. Granted that greed is bad from the standpoint of social justice, why is it bad business?

It's an illustration of the profit motive going out of control, to such a degree that the stockholders in a corporation—who are ultimately the owners—find that they are paying more money for less work being done by fewer people. The way this tends to happen, productivity and customer satisfaction decrease, and eventually profits shrink. Thus, the so-called "cost-cutting" manager or C.E.O. who had earned the respect of the stockholders ultimately becomes a liability. This sort of thing has a way of operating in cycles.

Unfortunately, the cost in terms of individual lives, between phases of the cycles, can be tragically high sometimes. What complicates the whole issue, too, is the fact that we now tend to live in a "global village," as I mentioned previously. A company headquartered in New York or Tokyo or Toronto sees itself as a corporate citizen of the world, oftentimes, and does not measure itself against the expectations and needs of a community where it opens up or shuts down a branch in a place somewhere in the southern or midwestern United States or in a developing nation in South America.

Q. 78. How, then, can a society fulfill all of the needs of the people when unbridled capitalism is the basis for the economic system?

Maybe it can't, if the term "unbridled" is included there. Most thoughtful people who have considered capitalism have tended to envision it with some form of control, restraint or social responsibility.

Q. 79. Isn't capitalism the freedom for everyone to have a place in the market?

In theory, yes; in practice, many people fear that there isn't *room* enough in the marketplace, at least not at the upper levels, if capitalism is permitted to operate without any sense of restraint. What operates here is what economists call the principle of excess competition: when a particular product or service is successful, others try to imitate it, to the point of saturation; the market eventually floods. It goes almost without saying that such a situation can have disastrous consequences for investors and employees, among others. Capitalism by its nature tends to overproduce goods and services, just as communism historically has underproduced. This is the basic reality of having an uncontrolled economy as opposed to a controlled one. But in point of fact we have virtually no such thing as either pure capitalism or pure communism in the world economic arena today.

Most countries that once embraced communism on virtually a wholesale basis—China, Cuba, the former Soviet republics—now insist that at least some measure of capitalistic or free-market economics needs to be part of their system in order to make it work. Likewise, practically every capitalistic country in the world has some form or another of governmental manipulation to make sure that the peaks and valleys of a free-market economy don't become too extreme. In the United States this has happened ever since the early twentieth century, and especially since the great depression of the 1930s. So-called *laissez-faire* (or "hands-off") economic policy has been dead, essentially, since the end of the nineteenth century.

Without becoming too bogged down in the economic ins and outs of the situation, it is being recognized by more and more responsible parties around the world that something must be done to address problems of oversupply and undersupply, whether of goods, labor or whatever. At the same time, it is acknowledged that a practical response to such questions cannot be so abrupt as to solve some problems and create or aggravate worse ones. To refer again to Pope John XXIII in *Mater et Magistra:*

161. Justice and humanity demand that those countries which produce consumer goods, especially farm products, in excess of their own needs should come to the assistance of those other countries where large sections of the population are suffering from want and hunger. It is nothing less than an outrage to justice and humanity to destroy or to squander goods that other people need for their very lives.

162. We are, of course, well aware that over-production, especially in agriculture, can cause economic harm to a certain section of the population. But it does not follow that one is thereby exonerated from extending emergency aid to those who need it. On the contrary, everything must be done to minimize the ill effects of over-production, and to spread the burden equitably over the entire population [*op. cit.*].

It is of special interest to note that the above words were published in 1961, over a generation ago now. At that time there were a number of Roman Catholic commentators who took exception to the teachings of their pope, on the grounds that this was just one more example of the church attempting to have unwarranted authority in secular matters, which the clergy should stay out of. So I do not quote the papal letter as a "proof text" in order to settle any arguments—since I know that anyone who feels inclined to dismiss these words will do so very quickly—but simply to help illustrate what I think is the state of the question and the shape of the problem addressed.

Q. 80. Are you saying, then, that if people are influenced by a Christian, or Judaeo-Christian, or even generally religious ethic, they will argue for some control of a capitalistic economy for the sake of the common good?

That is *exactly* what I am saying. We have already considered some of the ways in which this type of question has been viewed by religious teachings. We might look, also, at the famous image from the old poem by John Donne: "No man is an island." The point is that, as much as we like to think that every man and woman operates with autonomy, we all act within the context of social obligation to our neighbors. When we work for an employer, or employ a worker, or open or close a place of business, we perform actions which have an impact on the society around us, in a family, a neighborhood or a city, if not in a larger context as well. This is why we must be socially conscious of the potential effects of our actions, from not only an ethical point of view but also a business point of view in terms of relationships with communities and clienteles, at least locally and perhaps globally.

Part VII

———————————

Global Responsibility
and Business Ethics

Q. 81. We have already mentioned the fact that we now live and function, economically as well as otherwise, in a "global village." How does the sense of social obligation for one's own economic actions work out globally?

It has ramifications, I think, in a great many ways, of which we are not always aware. I like to remember the situation in which Gandhi found his people in India early in the twentieth century: they sold indigo dye to British clothing manufacturers, who had stopped buying it, and this resulted in the further impoverishment of the farmers in India. However, a great many Indians bought fabric, and finished clothing, from England since that was a ready source of supply. What Gandhi impressed upon them was the fact that when they did this they contributed to the misery of their own countrymen, if not themselves individually. So Gandhi led the people of India in a movement to spin their own fabric and make their own clothing. This is why the flag adopted by India upon its gaining independence from England bears the picture of a spinning wheel in its center.

Along the same lines, we might benefit from considering the words of theologian Brenda Consuelo Ruiz Perez, speaking at the World Council of Churches' seventh assembly at Canberra, Australia, in 1991:

> The cotton your clothes are made of may have come from Nicaragua, Guatemala or India.
>
> Your watch may be made with metals that perhaps came from Chile, Bolivia or Zaire.
>
> The coffee, bananas, cocoa and sugar that are part of your breakfast may have come from El Salvador, Colombia, Brazil or Kenya.

The medicines that some of you take may have ingredients that were taken out of our tropical forests.

The paper you use and the furniture you have in your home may have been made from wood that came from the rapidly disappearing forests in Costa Rica, Nigeria or Thailand (D. Preman Niles, comp., *Between the Flood and the Rainbow* [Geneva: WCC Publications, 1992], pgs. 52–53).

Q. 82. So what's the point of this—what are you suggesting in terms of social responsibility and business ethics?

What I'm suggesting is that the obligations of fair dealing go beyond the sorts of national boundaries we became so accustomed to during the eighteenth, nineteenth and twentieth centuries. Actually, the changing of such boundaries in dramatic fashion—typically as a result of war—should have been a clear signal, all along, that there were problems in the ways of the world economically. The world wars of the early twentieth century, the breakup of the Soviet Union and the subsequent chaos in parts of eastern Europe, the strife in Latin America and Africa—particularly Rwanda—are all indicative of that. If we do not have an equitable sharing in the production and consumption of the world's goods, we have not only social and economic imbalance but, ultimately, bloodshed and turmoil as a result.

Q. 83. Granted that the world's resources are in short supply and there is high demand, isn't this essentially a problem of over-population that needs to be addressed?

There are a great many people who would see the question in those terms, and they are sincerely concerned for the future of the world. But considerable evidence shows that it is not that simple. Late in 1994 the United Nations Conference on Population and Development met in Cairo and seemed to make that premise one of its operative pre-sumptions. But both the Roman Catholic Church and a significant num-ber of believers in other religions—especially Muslims—saw that position as a sort of "cop-out." It is true that in many parts of the world the supply of goods is far exceeded by the demand. However, what these Catholic, Muslim and other people of goodwill said is that the real problem lies in an inequitable distribution of those goods. This is not easy for me as an American to say, but the United States accounts for more consumption than either its production or its population would justify. The same could be said for some other industrially and technologically developed nations.

Q. 84. So are you saying that countries like the United States should somehow curtail economic consumption within their borders, thus limiting the market for other countries' goods and at the same time giving rise to greater unemployment and social unrest within North America?

Hardly. It is certainly possible to maintain the economies of the United States and other nations with a high level of consumption, but this can be done with the consumption spread abroad. One way to do this is with a pricing structure that is less prohibitive, in such areas as pharmaceuticals and medical technology in general. It can also be done in a variety of communication and service industries. But there is a price: the poor and the middle class can benefit only if those who are at the top of the economic pyramid—the C.E.O. types mentioned before—are willing to accept a degree of compensation which will still leave them well provided for but at a less conspicuous level of surplus.

Q. 85. At the same time, isn't a lot of "cheap labor" being imported into countries like the United States by virtue of immigration, with or without the benefit of legal documentation, and what are the implications of that kind of situation?

The implications are manifold. In 1994 we saw the beginning of a series of attempts to limit the rights of immigrants—first legal, then illegal—to certain benefits and services in various states of the union, beginning with California where "Proposition #187" was passed by the voters, although it later became embroiled in legal challenges on constitutional grounds. Some of the emotion behind that ballot measure certainly involved respect for "playing by the rules" and some of it involved irrational fears about "immigrants taking away our jobs" when a good many of the jobs in question would not be done by most people except immigrants in the first place. Moreover, the kind of law being enacted wanted to deny certain health and educational services to children who were hardly responsible for the immigration status of their parents. With all that, though, there is an important question: What is the essential difference between bringing people across the border (legally or illegally) to do a job cheaply and sending the job across the border to achieve the same result? In either case, the people doing the job accrue the same basic moral rights in exchange for their labor, even though the legalities of citizenship and certain entitlements will differ.

Q. 86. Will people simply accept this because the pope, or a group like the World Council of Churches, or anyone else, simply says so?

Obviously not. This is where some folks in positions of leadership have to read the "signs of the times" and perceive that a more equitable system of production, consumption and distribution is a good alternative to the sorts of destruction which came to its most alarming level during the twentieth century. One need not be a Nobel laureate in either economics or mathematics to know that the largest "third world" countries in terms of population are also among the poorest in the world, and have relatively little to lose in a war that employs the atomic weapons they now have developed, often with technology and materials somehow obtained from pioneer nuclear powers like the United States.

Q. 87. Do you think the situation would actually come to something like war?

I certainly hope not. But intelligent people have to consider the chance of it. I'm not just talking in the crude terms of so-called nuclear blackmail, but assessing the potential desperation of a society which cannot care for the people it has, and so feels some sense of relief in rallying them against a common enemy which they see as the cause of their misery. It has been done before, when the weaponry available was far less awesome and the loss of life was still considerable.

But once more we are drawn to the principle of enlightened self-interest. If those who have more of the world's goods than they ever could consume in a lifetime and more, for themselves and their families, would consider that their chance of preserving the bulk of what they have will actually be improved with a fairer sharing of the world's wealth, then perhaps we are on the way to a good start in this area.

Q. 88. Are you advocating communism, or a philosophy of "better red than dead"?

Not at all. It has been pointed out that communism places such limits on the human spirit as to dampen the kind of ambition which brings about the sort of discovery and growth necessary to sustain our population. This was noted by Pope John Paul II in his 1991 encyclical letter *Centesimus Annus*. It has also been observed in the virtual collapse of communism in most of the places where it was tried during the twentieth century, around the world, as we have noted previously. Even the celebrated life in common of the early Christians, documented briefly in the New Testament book of the Acts of the Apostles (2:41–47), shows that as time went on this kind of life left some things to be desired and gave rise to some problems. But, as John Paul II also pointed out, capitalism without limits is as dangerous as any other "ism" without limits. The free enterprise system does not succeed or endure as a "winner take all" game.

Q. 89. A great deal has been said about the role of countries like the United States and U.K. investing, in one way or another, in "third world" countries eager for economic development. But don't these nations themselves have some responsibility for the conditions under which they accept investment, in terms of protecting their environment and their workers?

Of course they do. A great difficulty arises, however, when the negotiations concerning the terms for investment do not take either the workers or the environment into account, but are conducted by affluent and powerful people on either side of the bargaining table. In effect, the same issues we have already discussed concerning the concept of "shareholders" applies throughout the world and across borders, as well as in one's own home area. Unfortunately, that sort of responsibility is not often realized and acted upon. There is, instead, the feeling that since a country is "underdeveloped"—at least by the standards of wealthier nations—that it is therefore going to be cooperative with almost any scheme to pump monies into its economy, and standards that might be insisted on elsewhere will be relaxed for the sake of expediency.

Q. 90. What obligation do we have to future generations regarding the development of resources and preservation of the environment?

There seems to be no responsible person today who denies such an obligation. In recent years there was a bumper sticker that was often seen on large cars driven by older people; it read: "We're spending our children's inheritance." Although that was an attempt at humor, many would acknowledge that such an attitude concerning environmental ethics had become prevalent in the twentieth century, even as danger signals began to sound concerning the ozone layer, the rain forests and global warming. The World Council of Churches, in the final document arising from its conciliar process of Mutual Commitment (Covenant) to Justice, Peace and the Integrity of Creation, affirmed that

> ...the land belongs to God. Human use of land and waters should release the earth to regularly replenish its life-giving power, protecting its integrity and providing spaces for its creatures...

And it committed its participants to

> ...protection and celebration of God's gift of creation by sharing the resources of the earth in ways that enhance the lives of all people...rejecting over-consumption and promoting models which encourage recycling, provide adequate shelter and appropriate transportation, provide sustainable forms of agricultural and industrial production, and meet the basic needs of all people...(quoted in Niles, comp., *op. cit.*, pgs. 174, 186).

Q. 91. Along the same lines, don't a lot of the wealthier nations in the world cause great damage to life and property by waging war in order to protect economic interests they have in other countries, and thereby commit a grave ethical offense?

The record of history would indicate that this has occurred often. Without analyzing all the data and evaluating its merit, suffice it to say that the defense of some parts of the world, in comparison to others, has been inconsistent at best, and may well be tied to the raw materials, labor or real estate available for direct or indirect exploitation by the "defenders" from more powerful nations. When this happens it is not unlike the wars of colonialism which helped build the great "empires" that seemed to reach their peak toward the end of the nineteenth century and had dwindled by the middle of the twentieth. But it does pose an ethical problem, when the "defense of freedom and human rights" in one part of the world seems far less crucial than in another, and the underlying reasoning seems at last to be economic. Assuming you consider the use of military force to be necessary in some cases, then the cases where it is applied show a disturbing inconsistency.

Q. 92. This raises another question, namely that of imperialism or colonialism. Is it morally, or ethically, right for one nation which is large and strong to take over the lands of indigenous peoples, or wouldn't it be better to allow those peoples to seek their own destiny?

The answer to that question is far more complex than the question itself implies, for many reasons.

It is undoubtedly true that there are some tribes or nations that have inhabited certain parts of the world for many centuries—most of Europe, Asia and Africa would be examples of this—with relatively little interaction with others, due to either geographic barriers (mountains, seas, etc.) or linguistic and cultural differences. During the twentieth century, though, many people were upset at the idea that some of the countries in those places demonstrated hostility toward immigrants or "foreigners" whom the natives saw as threatening them in terms of jobs or other opportunities (places to live, marriage, etc.). Yet some people who criticize this "xenophobia" seem equally insistent that people from Europe and the British Isles are "usurpers" in North America, while maintaining that people who have moved north from South America have merely followed a natural path of migration for economic opportunity. As the old saying has it, "Go figure!" A great deal of the rhetoric that began to be thrown around in the early 1990s, I believe, was but a smoke screen for the ambitions of certain groups or individuals who were determined to advance their own positions, and who chose what they considered persuasive forms of expression so as to make other groups or individuals feel guilty or intimidated. The fact is that all of us are indigenous to the places where we were raised, and all of us are somehow foreign to any other place we move to. As more and more interaction takes place between societies, then the blending of cultures comes about quite naturally, so that both Anglo and Latino children in some parts of New York learn to speak "Spanglish" in their neighborhoods, just as Parisians accommodate English words into the vocabulary of what is now called *Franglais*.

But the question before us now is whether or not a nation has a moral right to use force simply to conquer an area, as the Third Reich attempted to do during the 1930s and 1940s, so as to expand their own people's opportunities while subjugating others. Most people I know would respond to that sort of case in the negative. A few would argue that in some cases a superior culture or civilization is being brought to the fortunate residents of the territory being colonialized, and that force is necessary to overcome their ignorance of their good fortune. However, this latter view tends to strain the credibility of many rational people. Perhaps it is valuable here to observe that many nations, as they now are constituted, reflect past wars of imperialism or colonialism, but that the people who now live in them have developed a shared history and must work together to achieve their shared destiny in a beneficial way.

Q. 93. Should we even be talking about borders and nations at all, or is there an ethical obligation to move toward some sort of world government?

The kind of thing you are speaking of there could easily progress to a question of political methodology rather than one of ethical or moral concern. However, there is some bias in favor of allowing nations and various collections of peoples (clans, tribes or whatever name you wish) to choose and form their own associative bodies and structures, on at least a local level. This is implied in the "principle of subsidiarity" mentioned by Pope Pius XI in his social encyclical *Quadragesimo Anno* [1931]:

> 79. As history abundantly proves...it is an injustice...to assign to a greater and higher association what lesser and subordinate organizations can do. For every social activity ought of its very nature to furnish help to the members of the body social, and never destroy and absorb them.

Pope John XXIII made the same point, with specific reference to international relations, three decades later in *Pacem in Terris* [1963]:

> 141. ...It is no part of the duty of universal authority to limit the sphere of action of the public authority of individual states, or to arrogate any of its functions to itself. On the contrary, its essential purpose is to create world conditions in which the public authorities of each nation, its citizens and intermediate groups, can carry out their tasks, fulfill their duties and claim their rights with greater security.

Q. 94. Given the sort of thing just described, how effective can world bodies be in trying to bring about an ethical perspective in foreign policy decisions, especially when there are so many different cultures and religious or moral value systems around the world?

This sort of thing can hardly be expected to work perfectly, but I dare say we are doing better now than we did in the wake of some of the great wars of the nineteenth century and the early twentieth. Students of history know that the League of Nations, however idealistic its foundation, was no more effective in the long run than some of the alliances and treaties that had preceded it. Groups like the United Nations, and the Organization of American States, to use a couple of key examples, seem to have endured despite changes in geopolitics, perhaps because they are so inclusive of all the nations in their respective purviews, and cultivate a sense of common destiny, which results in the member nations' awareness of the need to act only after achieving consensus. In the eastern hemisphere, there will still be tensions between various sects within Islam, and between Muslims and other religious groups, in particular Hindus and Jews. As isolation eventually gives way to more social intercourse between these groups, this sort of tension will probably give way to understanding, though there is a good chance things will get worse before they finally get better.

Q. 95. There are good reasons for the sovereignty of individual nations, and for cooperation between them in a variety of international bodies, but for all that a serious problem still remains: How are we to deal with the burning or dumping of excess food supplies, so as to support prices in wealthier nations, while millions starve in other parts of the world?

If you are asking whether the situation you describe reflects acceptable moral or ethical conduct, the answer would have to be in the negative. Pope John XXIII wrote, in *Mater et Magistra:*

> 155. It is therefore obvious that the solidarity of the human race and Christian brotherhood demand the elimination as far as possible of these discrepancies. With this object in view, people all over the world must cooperate actively with one another in all sorts of ways, so as to facilitate the movement of goods, capital and men from one country to another...

If you are asking for a solution, then the situation becomes far more complex.

Part VIII

———————————

LOOKING FORWARD:
THE HINT OF A CONCLUSION

Q. 96. From your standpoint as a Christian educator, what can the church do in regard to some of these concerns?

At the risk of sounding pedantic, let me say that the church can do best in helping people realize and actualize ethical values in the economic sphere of human activity by being true to itself in terms of the four essential marks traditionally listed for the church: it must be *one, holy, catholic and apostolic.*

For the church to be one, it must resist the human temptation to be divided with bitterness over internal issues which are not matters of vital concern to the church. Examples of such things abound, but the point is made. We Christians have more things to bring us together than we have to divide us. This does not mean that a "one denomination fits all" sort of artificial ecumenism should prevail, wherein Lutherans, Roman Catholics, Baptists and Eastern Orthodox can all lose the special characteristics of their vital traditions, but it does mean that the body of Christ in the world needs to be one in pursuing social justice. This has already been done in some dramatic instances, like the civil rights movement in the United States during the middle of the twentieth century. And such unity of purpose, even with diversity of denominational structures, can be achieved again and again. Yet there are symbols of division that are hardly edifying. As a case in point, it is amazing that the World Council of Churches should approach its centennial without full membership and participation by the Church of Rome.

For the church to be holy is to achieve its most difficult task, for we are all sinners. But even with that realization, congregations and denominations have allowed some truly inappropriate leaders to flourish, to scandalize and to victimize. This sort of thing came to the fore in the 1980s when it became known that some fundamentalist Protestant "televangelists" were involved in swindling their contributors financially, and in some cases also guilty of sexual impropriety. In the 1990s, there emerged a series of horror stories about some clergy in more traditional denominations—especially Roman Catholic—who did much the same, despite a seminary system that had appeared to have been relatively "selective." Also, as the 1990s dawned, it became clear in retrospect that at least one celebrated religious leader during the twentieth century, while making great strides for social justice, was guilty of marital infidelity. Granted that such behavior on the part of a great and prophetic personality may be but an aberration, and granted that malfeasance on the part of ordained clergy occurs less frequently than in other professions, such things still do nothing to help and a good deal to harm the credibility of those who take up the banner of ethical conduct in the name of religion, and this is a concern that must somehow be dealt with. Also, if the church is to be truly "holy" it must strive for ways in which to make clearly visible its own commitment to the social and economic justice it proclaims to the world around it, ensuring that justice for those who are its own employees, whether in or outside of formal ordained ministry or religious order life.

For the church to be catholic (meaning universal) it must devote itself to preserving what Christians under the Holy Spirit have always believed and done at all times and in all places. This means concentrating on essentials, and avoiding those particularities which would have us cut off or separated from the mainstream of the church (*haeresis* is a Greek word which applies here, from which the term "heresy" comes when it involves matters of belief; "schism" more properly applies when the division is essentially one of authority or structure only). Once more, to put it simply, Christians have better enemies to fight in the world than one another, and need to save the energy involved for the battles that are truly worth waging.

For the church to be apostolic means for its members to be truly messengers (*apostoloi*) after the fashion of and with the zeal of those legendary first twelve, eager to touch the people and places with which the church is in contact, even at the expense of the incidentals of an immense institution. This will require, specifically, the rejection of *Caesaropapism,* that oft-repeated sort of alliance between the powerful leaders of a religion with those of a state, to the mutual benefit of the parties involved but to the detriment of the larger society around them and with great danger to the integrity of religion and state alike. It will mean a prophetic energy bent on making the world more in the image of God who created it in the first place, as an excellent way of showing gratitude for that gift and—especially among Christians—for the gift of the word of God taking on the nature of humanity. This is essentially what the apostle Paul had in mind in exhorting people to take seriously their roles as members of the body of Christ in the world, as mentioned in the New Testament epistles (1 Cor 12–13, Eph 4–5). Theologian William C. Spohn puts it this way:

> I want to propose that the entire story of Jesus is normative for Christian ethics as its concrete universal. It is not the only norm, because human nature, practical effectiveness, accurate descriptions of data, and the accumulated wisdom of the tradition are also normative. Nevertheless, whatever actions and dispositions these other sources suggest at least must be compatible with the basic patterns inherent in the story of Jesus. In addition, Jesus as concrete universal may urge certain actions and dispositions, like forgiveness of enemies, to which the other sources might not attach the same importance. Jesus functions normatively in Christian ethics through the paradigmatic imagination and moral discernment, which are distinctive ways of exercising moral authority....No abstract formula, however, can epitomize Jesus of Nazareth because his significance inheres in a particular life. The truth which he discloses has universal significance which comes not by way of theory or logical necessity but by plunging into the depths of the particulars. His meaning is inseparable from his story; it resides in the full range of encounters, personalities, and deeds which the Gospels relate (in "Jesus and Ethics," *Proceedings,* CTSA, 49:46).

Q. 97. That sounds very good, in terms of the church. But, as you have acknowledged previously, many people of faith are disillusioned by or somehow disconnected from the institutional

church with which they once identified. How do such people live and work as members of the church—the "body of Christ" in the world?

A Catholic lay leader I have known for years addressed this subject not long ago in a troubled city, during a time of great turmoil there which involved the closing of many Catholic schools and parish churches against the background of devastating sexual and financial scandals, of the kind that had plagued and disheartened some Protestant communities a few years prior. After having dedicated all his adult life to helping Catholic institutions raise funds, this man remarked that perhaps the twenty-first century will be the century of the Holy Spirit in the lives of Catholic individuals and families. He meant that after the initial shocks of the 1990s, these people would continue to live lives of Christian faith and action, but would not be crippled by discord or disarray on the part of the organizational church since they would be less dependent upon it. I don't mean to suggest that his perspective is anticlerical or separated from the official church, but simply that people have to get on with their lives of faith and justice as Christians whether or not they feel the support of the institution which they had become accustomed to when they were younger and the world was simpler. Perhaps this is a part, and a price, of growing up, when we realize that the "big people" we relied on as children cannot protect us as once we felt they would, and we are in many ways on our own.

Q. 98. If people are to be less dependent on institutional structures with which they had become comfortable, then what is to inspire or energize them and provide a source of moral leadership for them as Christians?

To refer once more to the Pauline vision of the church in the New Testament, we see that there is a strong community whose members support each other (*koinonia,* in the Greek of the New Testament) but that the body does not live without Jesus at its head. The epistles make this clear in sacramental terms (specifically baptism and eucharist). But it is also necessary for Christians to stress the person of Jesus as a source of Christian vision and wisdom to be applied to the world in which we live. While the church does well to stress the presence of Jesus among his people in the liturgy of the sacraments, there is increased awareness that this presence comes also through a serious and sustained contemplation of the word of God in the gospels.

Q. 99. How can people understand the teachings of Jesus and the meaning of his actions from the bible?

By this is not meant simply a literalistic "isogetic" approach to the bible, as though it were a series of "proof texts" based on direct quotes from the Lord (as in the traditional Protestant approach of the so-called "Red Letter Edition"), but rather an understanding of the Christian message in context, which can be illustrated and applied by such church teachings (the pope, the World Council of Churches, etc.) as we have considered here.

Q. 100. Given the tendency of human nature to succumb to weakness, can these considerations of ethics and these exhortations to Christian or any other religious action make a real difference?

We have already seen that this has been done many times in history, and at this point in time there is yet another opportunity—and an obligation—for men and women of religious faith or moral vision to at least make an effort.

Q. 101. We have been discussing the state of business or economic ethics at the end of the twentieth century. What do you see as the state of affairs a hundred years from now, at the end of the twenty-first—or even in fifty years, in the middle of the twenty-first?

While anything could happen in that span of time, I am optimistic. The explosion of human knowledge, just since the end of the nineteenth century, and the rapid expansion of communications media in the twentieth, have in the long run done more so far for good than for evil, and have helped us find some technological, economic, political and social solutions to a good deal of human misery and injustice.

There is greater awareness today than ever before of how our fellow human beings live around the world, and of what some of the important questions are. Moreover, there is greater understanding and appreciation of the various cultures and belief systems that influence men and women all over the world, coupled with a greater respect for them all. In this kind of atmosphere, steps forward can and will be taken. And even though the sense of "crowding" and social upheavals of various kinds will make some people feel compelled to do irrational and fearful things in defense of their own positions, I believe that at any given point in time, fifty or a hundred years from now, we human beings—with all our faults and failings—will show ourselves to have made a good deal of progress in terms of the ethics of the marketplace.

REFERENCES

Catechism of the Catholic Church
    (Vatican City: Libreria Editrice Vaticana, 1994)

Crook, Roger H.
    An Introduction to Christian Ethics, 2nd Edition
    (Englewood Cliffs, NJ: Prentice-Hall, 1995)

Devine, George
    American Catholicism: Where Do We Go From Here?
    (Englewood Cliffs, NJ: Prentice-Hall, 1975)

————
    The Seven Deadly Sins
    (Los Angeles: Twin Circle Publishing, 1988)

Hoffman, W. Michael and Frederick, Robert E.
    Business Ethics: Readings and Cases in Corporate
    Morality, 3rd Edition
    (New York: McGraw-Hill, 1995)

Johnson, Roger A. and Wallwork, Ernest, et al., eds.
    Critical Issues in Modern Religion
    (Englewood Cliffs, NJ: Prentice-Hall, 1990)

MacKinnon, Barbara
    Ethics: Theory and Contemporary Issues
    (Belmont, CA: Wadsworth, 1995)

Marthaler, Berard L.
Introducing the Catechism of the Catholic Church
(Mahwah, NJ: Paulist Press, 1994)

Niles, D. Preman, Comp.
Between the Flood and the Rainbow
(Geneva: WCC Publications, 1992)

Pelikan, Jaroslav, ed.
The World Treasury of Modern Religious Thought
(Boston: Little, Brown & Co., 1990)

Poole, Joyce
The Harm We Do
(Mystic, CT: Twenty-Third Publications, 1993)

Shaw, William H., and Barry, Vincent
Moral Issues in Business, 6th Edition
(Belmont, CA: Wadsworth, 1995)

Sloyan, Gerard S.
Catholic Morality Revisited
(Mystic, CT: Twenty-Third Publications, 1990)

Vanderhaar, Gerald
Why Good People Do Bad Things
(Mystic, CT: Twenty-Third Publications, 1994)

Walsh, Michael and Davies, Brian, eds.
Proclaiming Justice and Peace
(Mystic, CT: Twenty-Third Publications, 1991)

Westley, Dick
Morality and Its Beyond
(Mystic, CT: Twenty-Third Publications, 1992)

GLOSSARY

The following terms are used without elaboration in the preceding text, and with some frequency in either the regular communication of the business world or that of religious studies, but not necessarily in the everyday speech of the average person; working definitions of them are offered below:

accrue: build up or accumulate over a period of time.

asset: something of value owned by a person or corporation, including the right to collect sums of money in the future ("accounts receivable") or the expectation of business from a given community in the future ("goodwill").

bible: literally, from the Greek, "the book," containing the sacred writings of the Hebrew scriptures ("Old Testament") considered inspired by God for both Jews and Christians, and the Christian scriptures ("New Testament") likewise revered by Christians.

boycott: sometimes nicknamed a "consumers' strike"; the refusal of members of the public to buy goods or services from a particular individual or company, usually as a tactic to bring about a change in policy or to protest a form of behavior being engaged in by that individual or company.

brand names: familiar marketing labels used for products and services which are meant to be recognized by customers, and distinguished from their competitors; typically registered with governmental agencies, so as to avoid duplication, as "trademarks" or "service marks."

Buddha: literally "the enlightened one," Siddhartha Gautama, whose teachings over the centuries have remained central in the religious and ethical consciousness of millions in Asia and other parts of the world.

capital: purchasing power (money) which is not converted, and not likely to be converted soon, to goods or services. To have capital grow in value over time is the process of **capitalization,** and this takes place by lending the capital to others at a rental rate or rate of return (capitalization rate or **interest**); the underlying philosophy of this approach is called **capitalism**.

Caveat emptor: literally, "Let the buyer beware!" from the Latin; used commonly as part of the English language in business and legal circles to imply that a buyer has no recourse after considering and making a purchase.

C.E.O.: chief executive officer of a corporation or other business.

chains: series of locations for a single business, all marketing goods or services under the same name and general approach. Sometimes different "chain stores" are owned by different persons under a "franchise" agreement.

collective bargaining agreement (CBA): a contract made between a single employer (see below) and a number of employees (also below) whose relationship implies one or more factors in common, typically negotiated by representatives on the part of each side, often a union or association acting in behalf of the employees.

communism: a philosophy and an economic approach popular in the twentieth century, especially in eastern Europe and Asia, traced primarily to Karl Marx (thus also called **Marxism**). In direct opposition to capitalism (see above), communism rests on the principle "from each according to his means, to each according to his needs," with the state controlling the economy so as to bring about a "classless society" and achieve levels of production determined by advance planning.

compensation: consideration (see below) paid to someone in exchange for labor, in an employment relationship, including but not limited to the payment of money ("wages"); non-money compensation usually falls into the area of "(fringe) benefits" (typically paid vacation or sick leave, medical and/or dental insurance).

competitors: different persons or companies striving for the same compensation or opportunity within an economic system. From this comes the adjective **competitive**, meaning that one's marketing strategy is intended to be attractive in comparison with those of competitors; also related is the noun **competition**, meaning the process or act of seeking the same opportunities and rewards as others.

Confucius: Latinized name of Kung-fu-tzu ("Kung the teacher"), whose principles have formed the basis of religion and ethics for centuries in east Asia, especially China.

contract: a legally binding promise, made by two or more parties, to do or refrain from doing a certain thing, often for the purchase of goods or services in exchange for something of value ("**consideration**"); to be binding a contract must be made between parties who are capable of making a contract (sane adults, thus having "**capacity**") to do something which is possible and permissible by law (having a "**legal object**") and who, freely, have arrived at a "meeting of the minds" ("**mutual consent**").

corporations: organizations which have a legal identity that extends beyond that of a human being, although a human being may sometimes also become "incorporated"; typically, corporations which conduct business for a profit issue stock so that various parties may invest in the corporation without participating in its day-to-day operations. A corporation is called a "legal person" as distinct from a human being who is a "natural person."

covenant: agreement or promise, sometimes suggested by the acts of the parties as in "good faith covenant," which means that the parties are acting honestly and fairly with regard to one another.

employees: individuals who work for an agreed rate of compensation for a person or company (**employer**), usually considered entitled to a certain steady pattern of duties and compensation as the result of an oral or written contract, or by the force of an historical pattern, therefore usually unable to be dismissed without just cause according to the laws of most places.

encyclical (letters): in the Roman Catholic Church, documents circulated (thus the name "encyclical") by the bishop of Rome (pope) to his fellow bishops, concerning matters of doctrinal or pastoral importance, sometimes addressed directly to a wider audience (all Catholics, or the world as a whole), and called "social encyclicals" when dealing with issues in the socio-economic order; can be, but generally are not, vehicles for the pope's proclamation of a doctrine (dogma) relying on the "infallibility" of the church which may be exercised by the pope with his fellow bishops or acting alone.

Hinduism: religion common for centuries in the Indus valley region (India), emphasizing the lasting effect of one's deeds (**karma**); its chief writings are the **upanishads** and the **vedas.**

indentured servitude: a relationship combining some aspects of **employment** (see above) and **slavery** (see below), in which a person is obliged to work for a stated period of time for someone who provides some initial benefit (typically passage to a work site which is more desirable than the place the worker had left), thus the expression "working off one's indenture," after which the worker is free to seek employment in the service of another.

Koran: also called **Qu'ran,** the written doctrines of Islam as revealed through the prophet Muhammad.

"laissez-faire": an economic doctrine, especially popular in parts of Europe and the United States in the nineteenth century, which called for little or no governmental control or interference in a capitalistic economy.

liability: financial obligation or debt, including those that come due at some point in the future ("accounts payable").

merger: the combining of two businesses into one, whether the two are engaged in the same area of activity (like Price Club and Costco, two wholesale-warehouse stores, in the 1990s) or two different activities (like American Broadcasting Company and Paramount Pictures in the 1950s).

"moonlighting": the act of an employee taking on employment for more than one employer during the same general period of time (such as a "night job" when one has a "day job"), sometimes explicitly prohibited by certain employment contracts.

municipal: belonging or pertaining to the smallest civic unit of government, typically a city, town, village, township or borough, and sometimes a county, but not a larger structure such as a state or nation.

probationary period: stated time during which one must "prove oneself" (from the Latin), typically in employment. See **tenure**, below.

purveyors: providers or sellers of goods or services.

"restraint of trade": a legal concept which involves some interference with the conduct of business in a free market; generally opposed by public policy.

retirement (benefits): a form of compensation for employees which allows them to receive monies or wages from an employer after they have ceased working for that employer, generally on condition that the employee has completed a certain time period of service and/or a certain age in years; some employees fund their own retirement through a variety of programs (essentially, savings), and the Social Security programs of the U.S. government are an application of this principle.

slavery: a relationship in which one human being is the personal property ("chattel") of another, for purposes of work; slaves typically receive no monetary compensation for their labor but are given minimal food and housing by their "masters." Often slaves are prohibited from marrying without their masters' specific permission, and are sometimes expected to be available for the sexual pleasure of their "owners." This practice, often based on racial differences, was well known in various ancient civilizations like Greece and Rome, and in parts of the United States until the early 1860s.

stockholders: individuals or corporations who have loaned money to a corporation by purchasing shares of stock (thus a partial interest) in the corporation, in exercising the theory and practice of capitalism (see above).

takeover: the purchase by one business of another, with the purchasing business becoming the owner of the other and responsible for continuing or discontinuing its former activities (such as Bank of America "taking over" Gibraltar Savings in the 1980s); when this occurs through stock purchases against the wishes of the business being acquired, it is called a "hostile takeover."

Taoism: religious insights based on the Tao (pronounced "dow"), or **Tao te Ching** ("the way of the gods" or "the way and its power"), popularized through a wise teacher named **Lao-tzu** (also rendered **Lao-tse**).

tenure: the contractual right of a worker to expect continued employment for a certain minimum period of time—sometimes for the rest of his or her working life—provided a "probationary period" (see above) has been completed successfully and no just cause for termination occurs; this is best known in the teaching profession according to certain standards such as the 1940 "Statement of Principles on Academic Freedom and Tenure" of the American Association of University Professors (AAUP).

"trade secret": information learned by an employee in the service of an employer, thus considered the property of the employer and unable to be used by the employee except at the direction of or with the permission of the employer; typically the subject of a contract between employer and employee.

"wrongful discharge": the termination by an employer of an employee's contract without just cause, often alleged in lawsuits whether the contract is in writing or its elements are able to be known by a series of oral agreements and/or patterns of continued behavior.

Other Books in the Series